WILLIAMS-SONOMA

MASTERING

Sauces
Salsas & Relishes

Author
RICK RODGERS

General Editor
CHUCK WILLIAMS

Photographer
MARK THOMAS

NEW YORK · LONDON · TORONTO · SYDNEY

Contents

About this book

Mastering Sauces, Salsas & Relishes offers every reader a cooking class in book form, a one-on-one lesson with a seasoned teacher standing by your side, explaining each recipe step-by-step, with plenty of photographs to illustrate every detail.

Because sauces play integral yet different roles in so many dishes, it is important for the home cook to gain a thorough understanding of them. Some sauces need to be made in advance of a meal so they can rest before serving, letting flavors marry. Some should be served as soon as possible before an emulsion separates. Others need to be made from the juices of the food they will accompany. Once you have cooked your way through *Mastering Sauces, Salsas & Relishes,* you will have gained experience with every kind of basic sauce and will have become a confident cook who can whip up nearly any sauce a menu demands: a perfectly smooth hollandaise, a fragrant pesto, a meaty brown sauce, or a zesty salsa.

Here's how this book comprises a complete beginning course on sauces: The opening pages provide an overview of the different types of sauces, from traditional French béchamel to modern barbecue sauce. You'll get information on key tools, equipment, and ingredients, plus the basics on cooking, seasoning, and serving sauces. The Basic Recipes chapter shows you how to make a quartet of homemade stocks, the building blocks of many sauces, that you will use to create the recipes in subsequent chapters. The Key Techniques chapter teaches you the specific cooking skills needed to excel at making sauces, from clarifying butter and whisking a roux to fixing a broken sauce. Finally, the sauce recipes are grouped into three chapters according to how they are made.

With this cookbook in hand, you are well on your way to mastering the art of making sauces, one of the hallmarks of the accomplished home cook.

Working with the Recipes

Sauces are versatile elements of a meal and can be prepared in a variety of ways that fit into virtually every lifestyle or occasion, from casual everyday dining to the most formal dinner party. But before you are ready to serve a delicious sauced dish to your friends or family, you need to develop the skills to make sauces with confidence. The organization of the recipes in this book will help you to learn those key skills, and then build on them.

Each recipe chapter is anchored by at least one master recipe, which takes you through a classic sauce recipe step-by-step, with both words and pictures. I suggest tackling these key skill-building recipes first. You'll find it's like having a cooking teacher or chef in the kitchen with you as you cook.

After you work through the master recipes, the other recipes will help you to continue your learning. Guided by photos illustrating any confusing or difficult aspects of the other recipes, you

will build your sauce-making confidence as you continue your way through the book.

As any accomplished cook will tell you, the secret behind success is practice. If you are a novice, a recipe may not turn out the way you expected and may take longer to make than you imagined. But as you learn to work more comfortably and efficiently, that same recipe will come more naturally each time you make it, and you'll develop speed. Remember, any time you spend in the kitchen is an investment in your skills.

Recipe variations provide another way to hone your cooking expertise and build a repertory of sauces. For example, once you learn how to make classic Hollandaise Sauce (page 81), you'll have the skills necessary to prepare Sauce Maltaise (page 86) or Béarnaise Sauce (page 87) by merely changing a few ingredients. You'll find such variations of classic recipes throughout the book.

You won't need special equipment to make sauces. The essentials are outlined on pages 130–33.

Types of Sauces

Until relatively recently, sauces were categorized according to the classical French system, popularized in the early nineteenth century by Antonin Carême. This master chef identified five main recipes—béchamel, espagnole, hollandaise, tomato, and velouté—as the "mother sauces" from which myriad variations were born. Today's cooks, however, are just as likely to crave Indian chutney or Italian pesto as one of these traditional French choices.

This book divides sauces into three general classifications according to how they are prepared.

Pan Sauces & Reduction Sauces

The drippings left in a pan after sautéing or roasting can be transformed easily into a pan sauce. Depending on the ingredients used, the result can be light and delicate, or savory and rich like gravy. In similar sauces, a liquid is thickened, sometimes with the aid of a starch, by boiling it down, or *reducing* it.

Emulsions & Butter Sauces

Emulsion sauces include hollandaise, mayonnaise, and vinaigrette. The thick, smooth body of an emulsified sauce is the effect of blending a fat (most often melted butter or olive oil) and a liquid (such as lemon juice or vinegar) that don't normally combine into a delicate balance. In a butter sauce, butter is warmed and softened while being mixed with other flavors to create a semiliquid sauce with a uniquely creamy texture.

Salsas, Purées & Relishes

This group is often characterized by the use of fresh fruit, vegetables, or herbs. Usually not wedded to French culinary tradition, these casual, flavorful, and quickly prepared sauces come from the cuisines of many other cultures.

Choosing a Sauce

The variety of sauces in the chapters that follow allows you to select one that is ideal for the menu or season at hand.

When choosing a sauce, there are usually three general considerations. Quite often, the desired effect is to echo the flavors of the main ingredient: for instance, saucing a seafood dish with a delicate velouté made with fish fumet. Or, sometimes a counterpoint is the goal: sharp, smooth cheese sauce over plain, crisp vegetables. Another option is matching two rich components: poached eggs topped with lush hollandaise come to mind. All the recipes in this book include recommended uses to guide you in the correct direction.

Mood and seasonality are other considerations. Pan sauces are quick to make, perfect for a weeknight meal, while gravies require lots of drippings from a slow-cooking roast, de rigueur for a holiday feast. There's a sauce for any time of year: you'll want a barbecue sauce for a midsummer cookout, and a white sauce for a midwinter root-vegetable gratin. Peach chutney and cranberry relish show off seasonal produce and are all you need to dress up simple grilled or roasted meat or poultry.

Understanding Sauce Ingredients

A sauce will turn out only as good as the ingredients that go into it. High-quality ingredients—vegetables and fruits in season and at their peak of flavor, fragrant herbs and spices that are not past their prime, first-class cheeses—are a must. Sometimes the difference is crucial: old butter that has picked up flavors from the refrigerator can ruin a hollandaise or beurre blanc, and a thin-bodied wine will deprive a béarnaise sauce of its proper character.

Pan & Reduction Sauce Ingredients

Homemade stock, which is made by simmering meat and bones in water with aromatic ingredients, is the foundation of this group of sauces. Homemade stock gives the cook more control over the seasoning and quality of the finished sauce. Get in the habit of making stock on a lazy weekend and freezing the fruits of your labor. If you must use store-bought stock, choose a reduced-sodium brand. To improve the flavor, mix with an equal amount of water, about

½ pound (250 g) of the bones of an appropriate meat (wings for chicken or a marrowbone for beef), and a chopped small onion and carrot, if you wish. Bring to a boil over high heat, skim off any foam, and add a pinch of dried thyme. Reduce the heat to low and simmer, uncovered, for an hour or so.

Milk and wine often supplement the stock in these sauces. Whole milk will give the best body; reduced-fat milk makes thin, translucent béchamel sauce. In general, avoid nonfat milk for making

sauces. For the best flavor in wine-based sauces, choose a hearty red, such as a Syrah, Zinfandel, or Cabernet Sauvignon, or a crisp, unoaked white, such as Sauvignon Blanc or Pinot Grigio.

For pan and reduction sauces, flour and cornstarch (cornflour) are the thickeners of choice. All-purpose bleached and unbleached (plain) flour are interchangeable as thickeners. Cornstarch is usually dissolved in liquid before using. Flour is typically combined with a fat to make a roux.

Emulsion & Butter Sauce Ingredients

Unsalted butter is usually fresher than salted (salt is added as a preservative). European-style butter has a tangier, richer flavor, thanks to the churning of high-butterfat, mildly fermented cream.

Egg yolks help emulsify the fats (oil or butter) and liquids (lemon juice or vinegar) of a hollandaise or mayonnaise; use large Grade A eggs. *Note: Uncooked eggs can carry salmonella, a bacterium that can cause serious illness, and should not be served to very young or elderly people or those with compromised immune systems. If these conditions apply to you, search out pasteurized eggs, which have been exposed to a high temperature to kill bacteria.*

Salsa, Purée & Relish Ingredients

Keep two words in mind when making these produce-based condiments: fresh and flavorful. Bruised fruits, flabby vegetables, and wilted herbs will give a sauce poor flavor that all the seasoning in the world cannot disguise. Keep seasonality as a foremost consideration. For example, in winter, make Orange-Rosemary Salsa (page 119) from ripe oranges rather settling for mealy, pale, out-of-season tomatoes to make the Tomato Salsa (page 117).

Flavorings for Sauces

From the onion family, shallots, leeks, and garlic contribute their aromatic flavors to countless sauces. They should be firm and unblemished.

Cheese shows up in classic pesto and cheese sauces. In general, use the best available types, such as nutty Gruyère when Swiss is called for, or aged farmstead Cheddar. There is only one true Parmesan cheese, the famous Parmigiano-Reggiano of northern Italy, which should be freshly grated just before use. Parmigiano-Reggiano is recommended for these recipes.

Use fresh herbs whenever possible. Be sure to wash and thoroughly dry them before using. A salad spinner makes quick work of this process.

Dried herbs and spices should be used within six months of purchase, as they lose flavor with age. Freshly ground spices, including pepper, will give the best-tasting results.

There are many types of salt on the market today—table salt, sea salt, and kosher salt being the most common—and they all have different-sized crystals, so they measure differently. The recipes in this book were tested using fine-grain sea salt, which dissolves easily in sauces.

Cooking, Seasoning & Serving Sauces

Many sauces can be made slightly ahead of serving time. But even when a sauce requires last-minute attention, a bit of organization will take the stress out of the finishing touches. As in all cooking, making sauces involves the senses. You must learn to judge if the sauce at hand is thick enough or has the proper amount of seasoning to please both the eye and the palate. This talent can come only from patience and long, steady practice.

Mise en Place

The French culinary term *mise en place* refers to having everything "in its place" before actual cooking begins. Regardless of your skill level, this is an invaluable habit to cultivate, as it saves time and avoids confusion. Before you begin to follow the method of a recipe, make sure all needed tools and cookware are ready at hand and use the information in the ingredient list to prepare and measure out each item exactly as described. Pay attention to syntax: "1 cup walnuts, chopped" and "1 cup chopped walnuts" are not the same thing. (The former asks for whole nuts to be measured, then chopped, and the latter asks for a measure of already-chopped walnuts.) If necessary, refrigerate ingredients that should be used chilled in the recipe, or remove refrigerated ingredients to bring them to room temperature as needed.

A Guide to Measuring

Inaccurate measurements can spell disaster in the kitchen, especially with sauces, which rely on a carefully balanced mixture of ingredients. For example, if the liquid in an emulsified sauce is a teaspoon off, the sauce may not bind, and an extra tablespoon of flour in a roux will render a sauce too thick.

DRY INGREDIENTS Most professional bakers prefer the "spoon and sweep" method for measuring dry ingredients like flour, which starts by spooning the ingredients into a dry measuring cup. However, for the smaller amounts required for sauces, the more casual "dip and sweep" method works well: dip the measuring cup or spoon into the ingredient, then sweep off the excess with the dull edge of a knife so that the ingredient is level with the edge of the cup. For ingredients such as basil leaves, pack the item firmly into the cup.

LIQUID INGREDIENTS Always use a transparent liquid measuring cup and take the reading at eye level. Such cups have room at the top to prevent overflow and a pour spout for the smooth addition of any liquid to a sauce.

BUTTER Most butter wrappers are conveniently marked with tablespoon and cup increments: simply cut off the amount you need from the stick.

Preheating Ovens & Pans

Browning foods gives them an appealing color and depth of flavor. An oven temperature that is too low or a pan that is improperly heated hinders the browning process. Deeply browned bones are essential for a rich stock, one of the key ingredients in many sauces.

Every oven should have an oven thermometer to indicate the true temperature, as built-in thermostats can go awry. Allow at least 15 minutes to preheat an oven to 350°F (180°C), and longer for higher temperatures.

For panfried meats and poultry, surface browning is highly desirable for flavor. The pan should be well heated over medium-high to high heat before the food is added, ensuring that the food begins to brown as soon as it makes contact with the pan. A refined oil (such as pure olive oil) or a light-bodied vegetable oil (such as canola oil) is usually used as the cooking fat when panfrying, as milk solids in butter will burn at such temperatures, and the flavor of an extra-virgin olive oil will be ruined.

The Cooking Process

The cook's most valuable tools are his or her own senses. The best meals are not made with a stopwatch. Consider the recommended cooking times in a recipe as guidelines, not rules. Some of the many variables that affect cooking times include the material and thickness of a pan and the pan's ability to absorb heat, the age of the ingredients and their temperature before cooking, and the heat level of your stove top or oven.

In fact, because the cook must determine for him- or herself how the cooking is progressing, recipes do not always include precise timing for key steps. Mounting a beurre blanc with butter (see page 41) is not just an illustration of how an individual controls the cooking process, but of the old adage that practice makes perfect. The butter should be whisked into the base liquid one or a few pieces at a time, where it is slowly softened into a semiliquid state. The exact timing is impossible to establish. It is up to you to watch the mixture closely and adjust the heat of the burner to keep the butter from simply melting or, if necessary, to remove the saucepan from the heat entirely. As you continue to practice making a beurre blanc, incorporating the butter into the sauce will become second nature, and beurre blanc will become a familiar member of your cooking repertory.

Kitchen Safety

All perishable foods, including sauces, should be held for no more than 2 hours at room temperature or in a warm-water bath. Egg-based sauces are especially susceptible to bacterial growth.

Before refrigerating any sauce or stock, be sure it cools to room temperature so that you do not raise the temperature of the refrigerator and compromise other foods. To speed the cooling of a stock or sauce, transfer it to a bowl, and place the bowl in a larger bowl of ice water (this is called an ice bath). Let stand, stirring often, until cooled.

Methods of Thickening Sauces

The most common ways to thicken a sauce are reduction, mounting with butter, and using a slurry or a roux.

REDUCTION When you let a sauce cook, some liquid evaporates, the volume is reduced, and result is a thickened sauce and intensified flavor. For very thin liquids, such as stock that you want to reduce to a demi-glace, the sauce is boiled rapidly. Thicker sauces, such as velouté, should be simmered slowly. In either case, watch out for scorching.

MOUNTING WITH BUTTER When cold butter is whisked into a warm sauce base (such as the shallot-wine reduction of a beurre blanc), the butter slowly softens into a semiliquid consistency. The butter not only adds its delicious flavor, but it also increases the volume of—or mounts—the sauce. Mounting should be done off the heat or over very low heat, or the butter will quickly melt into a greasy liquid.

USING A SLURRY Cornstarch (cornflour) dissolved in a small amount of cold liquid is called a slurry. For easy dissolving, always add the cornstarch to the liquid (water, wine, or stock) and not the other way around, which can cause lumps. Small amounts of slurry can be whisked into a simmering sauce base, which is then brought to a boil and cooked until thickened as desired. (A slurry does not release its thickening power until it reaches the boiling point.) Add the slurry a little at a time, or the sauce can become too thick.

USING A ROUX Equal amounts of melted butter or other fat and flour, whisked together into a paste and cooked, is called a roux. White sauces use a roux that is cooked over low heat to a pale ivory color. To add deeper color and a toasted flavor to brown sauces, the roux is cooked longer until lightly browned. The darker the roux, the deeper its flavor, but the less thickening power it has.

Developing Your Seasoning Palate

Salt balances and brings out the flavors of other ingredients. Taste at different stages of cooking (as long as the sauce doesn't contain uncooked eggs or raw meat) to judge the saltiness. Add freshly ground pepper along the way, too, but use a light hand, since the sauce will accompany food that will likely already be seasoned.

Straining & Puréeing Sauces

Although many sauces seem relatively smooth at the end of cooking, they can be strained with a medium-mesh sieve or even a fine conical strainer, or *chinois,* for the silkiest texture.

The ingredients for puréed sauces are traditionally ground together in a mortar and pestle, resulting in a pleasantly rustic texture. A food processor is quicker and makes a smoother sauce, while a blender gives the smoothest result. In either case, stop the machine often and scrape down the sides of the container so that the ingredients are evenly combined.

Even a puréed sauce will benefit from a final straining. The Grilled Red Pepper Coulis on page 120 is a perfect example, as the initial purée of red peppers could be served as is, but a pass through a sieve gives it a refined elegance.

Serving Sauces

Once you have created a sauce, there are still many choices for how to serve it. For casual meals, you won't need more than a sauceboat. But for a more professional look, the sauce can be ladled, pooled, napped, or even squeezed through a plastic bottle for different results. No matter which method you choose, remember that a sauce is supposed to enhance the food, not drown it. If appropriate, finish each serving with a sprinkle of chopped herbs to provide a counterpoint of flavor and color.

LADLING A ladle not only controls portions, but keeps servings neat, allowing you to pour the sauce on the food with precision. For the best appearance, pour the sauce in a stream across the center of the food.

POOLING Often, a dish will look most attractive if a sauce is served underneath the food, instead of on top. In this case, ladle some sauce onto a plate, coaxing the sauce into an even pool with the rounded side of the ladle. Then place the main ingredient, such as a fish fillet or grilled steak, on top of the sauce.

NAPPING Cloaking the food with a wide sheet of sauce (in French, *nappe* means "cloth" or "sheet") is a method that works best with moderately thick sauces, such as Hollandaise Sauce (page 80). The shape of the food should be visible under its cloak of sauce. Cauliflower, broccoli, and asparagus are often sauced in this manner. A large metal serving spoon (about 4 inches/10 cm long and 2 inches/5 cm wide) allows the best control when applying the sauce over the food in a wide, even ribbon.

PIPING For an abstract look, use plastic squeeze bottles (the kind used to dispense condiments) to pipe the sauce in squiggles and zigzags on a plate. If necessary, thicken reduction sauces with a bit more cornstarch (cornflour) than usual so the design doesn't run all over the plate. Rub puréed sauces through a fine-mesh sieve so they are very smooth, or the ingredients may clog the bottle tip. Emulsified sauces are usually too thick or too delicate to squeeze through a bottle.

Chilling and Warming Plates

To keep cold sauces cold and warm sauces warm, plates and sauceboats should be chilled or warmed accordingly. Run each plate or the sauceboat under very cold or very hot water for a few seconds, then dry thoroughly. Alternatively, place them in the refrigerator or, if heatproof, in a very low (150°F/65°C) oven about 10 minutes ahead of serving time.

1

Basic Recipes

Making stocks is one of the first lessons in any cooking class. And because stocks are building blocks for countless sauces, mastering stock making is critical to successful sauce making. In this chapter, you will learn how to roast bones for brown stocks, how to skim stocks as they simmer, and how to defat meat and poultry stocks— all indispensable lessons in turning out good stocks.

For the bouquet garni

4 sprigs fresh flat-leaf (Italian) parsley

1 sprig fresh thyme

1 bay leaf

8 whole peppercorns

5 lb (2.5 kg) chicken backs or wings, or a combination

1 large yellow onion, peeled

1 large carrot

1 large stalk celery with leaves

2 tablespoons canola oil

2 cups (16 fl oz/500 ml) water, plus more to cover the stock ingredients

MAKES ABOUT 3 QT (3 L)

Brown Poultry Stock

If you are going to make and store only one stock, this is the one to choose. Cooked properly, it will be clear and golden yellow and have a rich chicken flavor. The bones are simmered in water just long enough to release their flavor and release their gelatin, lending good full body to the finished stock.

1 Make a bouquet garni

If you are not sure how to make a bouquet garni, turn to page 40. Wrap the parsley, thyme, bay leaf, and peppercorns in a piece of damp cheesecloth (muslin) and secure with kitchen string.

2 Chop the backs and wings

If you have a heavy cleaver, chop the backs into 2- to 3-inch (5- to 7.5-cm) pieces. This will help release the gelatin from the bones. Cut the wings at the joints: Place the cleaver or a heavy knife directly in the joint (bend the wing to find the spot) and press on the top of the knife with the heel of one palm.

3 Roast the chicken parts

Position an oven rack in the upper third of the oven and preheat to 425°F (220°C). (Allowing the heat to circulate underneath the pan will encourage even, deep browning of the bones.) Spread the chicken parts, overlapping them if necessary, in a very large roasting pan. A nonstick pan will work, but it's best not to use nonstick for this recipe; you want lots of browned bits to stick to the bottom of the pan—what chefs call a *fond*. Roast for 30 minutes. Using tongs, turn the chicken parts over and continue roasting until the pieces are deeply browned, about 20 minutes longer.

4 Sauté the vegetables

Meanwhile, coarsely chop the onion, carrot, and celery. Place a stockpot or large saucepan over medium-high heat. Add the oil and heat until the surface just shimmers. Add the vegetables and cook, stirring occasionally, until starting to brown, about 12 minutes.

5 Deglaze the roasting pan

Using tongs, transfer the browned chicken to the stockpot. Discard any fat in the roasting pan. To find out more about deglazing, turn to page 41. Place the roasting pan over 2 burners on high heat and heat until the juices sizzle. Pour the 2 cups water into the roasting pan. Bring to a boil, scraping up the browned bits on the bottom and sides of the pan with a wooden spatula or spoon.

6 Bring the stock to a boil

Pour the brown liquid into the pot, then add the bouquet garni. Add water to cover the ingredients by about 1 inch (2.5 cm); more water could dilute the flavor of the finished stock. Turn on the heat to high.

7 Simmer the stock

As soon as you see bubbles forming, reduce the heat to low. Skim off any foam from the surface with a large slotted spoon or skimmer. The foam is the impurities being released from the bones and meat; if not removed, it will cloud the stock. Let the stock simmer, regularly skimming any foam from the surface, until it is full flavored, at least 3 hours and up to 6 hours. Add additional water, if necessary, to keep the ingredients just covered. Watch that the stock doesn't come to a boil, or fat from the meat will be suspended in the stock, which will make it taste greasy.

8 Strain and defat the stock

Carefully pour the stock through a sieve lined with damp cheesecloth into a large tempered glass or stainless-steel bowl and discard the solids. Let the stock stand for 5 minutes, then carefully skim the clear yellow fat from the surface with a large metal spoon. Or, if time allows, fill a large bowl partway with ice water and set the stock in the ice bath to cool to room temperature, stirring occasionally. Cover and refrigerate overnight. The fat will rise to the top and solidify, making it easy to scrape it off the surface.

9 Store the stock

Cover the stock and refrigerate it for up to 3 days, or pour into airtight containers and freeze for up to 3 months.

CHEF'S TIP

It is a good idea not to season the stock until you are ready to use it. For example, if you are using it for a pan sauce, it could become overly salty through the process of reducing the liquid. To taste-test a stock to be sure it is sufficiently full flavored, I ladle a little of it into a cup, add a pinch of salt, and taste for a well-rounded flavor.

RECOMMENDED USES

In brown sauces for poultry or pork and for making pan sauces from roasted or sautéed poultry or pork.

Brown Meat Stock

Browning the bones and deglazing the pan drippings gives this kitchen staple its rich brown color. The small amount of meat on the bony cut of beef or veal will contribute extra flavor to the finished stock, which should have good body and intensely meaty flavor from long simmering.

For the bouquet garni

4 sprigs fresh flat-leaf (Italian) parsley

1 sprig fresh thyme

1 bay leaf

8 whole peppercorns

2½ lb (1.25 kg) veal soup bones or marrowbones, cut into chunks by the butcher

1 lb (500 g) bony cut of beef or veal such as beef shin or veal shank

1 large yellow onion, peeled

1 large carrot

1 large stalk celery with leaves

2 tablespoons canola oil

2 cups (16 fl oz/500 ml) water, plus more to cover the stock ingredients

MAKES ABOUT 3 QT (3 L)

1 **Make a bouquet garni**
If you are not sure how to make a bouquet garni, turn to page 40. Wrap the parsley, thyme, bay leaf, and peppercorns in a piece of damp cheesecloth (muslin) and secure with kitchen string.

2 **Roast the bones**
Position an oven rack in the upper third of the oven and preheat to 425°F (220°C). (Allowing the heat to circulate underneath the pan will encourage even, deep browning of the bones.) Spread the veal and beef bones and the shin or shank, overlapping them if necessary, in a very large flameproof roasting pan, preferably not nonstick. (You want browned bits to stick to the pan bottom for extra flavor.) Roast for 30 minutes. Using tongs, turn the pieces over and continue roasting until all the pieces are a rich mahogany brown, about 20 minutes longer.

3 **Sauté the vegetables**
Meanwhile, coarsely chop the onion, carrot, and celery. Place a stockpot or large saucepan over medium-high heat. Add the oil and heat until the surface just shimmers. Add the vegetables and cook, stirring occasionally, until starting to brown, about 12 minutes.

4 **Deglaze the roasting pan**
Using tongs, transfer the browned bones and meat to the stockpot. Discard any fat in the roasting pan. To find out more about deglazing, turn to page 41. Place the roasting pan over 2 burners on high heat until the juices sizzle. Pour the 2 cups water into the roasting pan. Bring to a boil, scraping up the browned bits on the bottom and sides of the pan with a wooden spatula or spoon.

5 Bring the stock to a boil

Pour the brown liquid into the pot, then add the bouquet garni. Add cold water to cover the ingredients by about 1 inch (2.5 cm); more water could dilute the flavor of the finished stock. Turn on the heat to high.

6 Simmer the stock

As soon as you see bubbles forming, reduce the heat to low. Skim off any foam from the surface with a large slotted spoon or skimmer. The foam is the impurities being released from the bones and meat; if not removed, it will cloud the stock. Let the stock simmer, regularly skimming any foam from the surface, until it is full flavored, at least 4 hours and up to 8 hours. Add additional water, if necessary, to keep the ingredients just covered. Watch that the stock doesn't come to a boil, or fat from the meat will be suspended in the stock, which will make it taste greasy.

7 Strain and defat the stock

Carefully pour the stock through a sieve lined with damp cheesecloth into a large tempered glass or stainless-steel bowl and discard the solids. Let the stock stand for 5 minutes, then carefully skim the yellow fat from the surface with a large metal spoon. Or, if time allows, fill a large bowl partway with ice water and set the stock in the ice bath to cool to room temperature, stirring occasionally. Cover and refrigerate overnight. The fat will rise to the top and solidify, making it easy to scrape it off the surface.

8 Store the stock

Cover the stock and refrigerate it for up to 3 days, or pour into airtight containers and freeze for up to 3 months. Chilled stock will have a gelatinous consistency; warm the stock until it "melts" before measuring.

CHEF'S TIP

When adding additional water to the stock to keep the ingredients covered, I like to use hot water. Adding cold water can cool the stock too much, causing it to stop simmering.

RECOMMENDED USES

In brown sauces for meats and for making pan sauces from roasted or sautéed meats.

White Stock

White stocks are used to make white sauces, so they should be neutral and delicate so as not to detract from the other flavors in the sauce. I like to combine chicken bones and veal bones, the first for flavor and the second for richness, but you could use all chicken or all veal bones if you prefer.

For the bouquet garni

4 sprigs fresh flat-leaf (Italian) parsley

1 sprig fresh thyme

1 bay leaf

8 whole peppercorns

1 large carrot

1 large stalk celery with leaves

1 large yellow onion

3 lb (1.5 kg) veal soup bones or marrowbones

2 lb (1 kg) chicken wings or backs, or a combination

MAKES ABOUT 3 QT (3 L)

1 Make a bouquet garni
If you are not sure how to make a bouquet garni, turn to page 40. Wrap the parsley, thyme, bay leaf, and peppercorns in a piece of damp cheesecloth (muslin) and secure with kitchen string.

2 Chop the vegetables
Use a vegetable peeler to peel the carrot, then switch to a chef's knife and cut the carrot crosswise into large pieces. Next, cut the celery into pieces about the same size as the carrot. Finally, cut the onion in half and peel it. Cut each onion half into large chunks.

3 Bring the stock to a boil
Combine the veal bones, chicken parts, carrot, celery, onion, and bouquet garni in a stockpot or large saucepan. Add water to cover the ingredients by about 1 inch (2.5 cm); more water could dilute the flavor of the finished stock. Turn on the heat to high.

4 Simmer the stock
As soon as you see bubbles forming, reduce the heat to low. Skim off any foam from the surface with a large slotted spoon or skimmer. The foam is the impurities being released from the bones and meat; if not removed, it will cloud

the stock. Let the stock simmer, regularly skimming any foam from the surface, until it is full flavored, at least 4 hours and up to 8 hours. Add hot water, if necessary, to keep the ingredients just covered. Watch that the stock doesn't come to a boil, or fat from the meat will be suspended in the stock, which can make it taste greasy.

5 Strain and defat the stock

Carefully pour the stock through a sieve lined with damp cheesecloth into a large tempered glass or stainless-steel bowl and discard the solids. Let the stock stand for 5 minutes, then carefully skim the yellow fat from the surface with a large metal spoon. Or, if time allows, fill a large bowl partway with ice water and set the stock in the ice bath to cool to room temperature, stirring occasionally. Cover and refrigerate overnight. The fat will rise to the top and solidify, making it easy to scrape it off the surface.

6 Store the stock

Cover the stock and refrigerate it for up to 3 days, or pour into airtight containers and freeze for up to 3 months. Chilled stock will have a gelatinous consistency; warm the stock until it "melts" before measuring.

CHEF'S TIP

Bundling the herbs as a bouquet garni keeps them from floating around in the stock and interfering with skimming. It also makes them easy to remove at the end of cooking, before straining.

RECOMMENDED USES

In velouté and velouté-based sauces or light pan sauces.

Fish Fumet

Stock is a long-simmered affair, so the quick-cooking version made with fish is not properly called a stock, but rather a *fumet*, from the French for "aroma." Because thin fish bones rapidly release their flavor into a simmering liquid, the fumet only becomes bitter with lengthy cooking.

1½ lb (750 g) fish heads and/or bones from white-fleshed, nonoily fish such as snapper, flounder, or halibut

For the bouquet garni

3 sprigs fresh flat-leaf (Italian) parsley

8 whole peppercorns

2 sprigs fresh thyme

¼ teaspoon fennel seeds

½ bay leaf

1 large leek, white and pale green part only

1 stalk celery

1 tablespoon canola oil

¾ cup (6 fl oz/180 ml) dry white wine such as Sauvignon Blanc or Pinot Grigio

MAKES ABOUT 1½ QT (1.5 L)

1 Clean the fish heads and bones

If you are using fish heads, lift up the flaps on either side of the head and use kitchen scissors to snip away the reddish brown gills (be careful, because the gills are sharp). Rinse the heads and bones well under running cold water, and use the tip of a sharp knife to remove any traces of viscera. Put the heads and bones in a large bowl and cover them with cold water. Let the fish parts soak for 15 minutes, then drain and rinse them again. Soaking the fish parts removes any remaining blood and viscera and makes a clearer, fresher-tasting stock.

2 Make a bouquet garni

If you are not sure how to make a bouquet garni, turn to page 40. Wrap the parsley, peppercorns, thyme, fennel seeds, and bay leaf in a piece of damp cheesecloth (muslin) and secure with kitchen string.

3 Prepare the vegetables

Cut the leek in half lengthwise. Fill a bowl or basin with water and wash the leek halves carefully, swishing them around and gently spreading the layers to remove any grit. Drain and shake the leeks well, then use a chef's knife to cut them into ½-inch (12-mm) dice. Next, cut the celery into halves or thirds. Cut each piece lengthwise into strips ½ inch (12 mm) wide. Line up the strips a few at a time and cut them crosswise into ½-inch (12-mm) dice.

  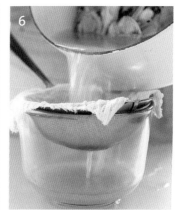 

4 **Sweat the vegetables**
Place a Dutch oven or other large saucepan over low to medium-low heat. Add the oil and heat until the surface just shimmers. Add the leek and celery and cover. Cook, stirring occasionally, until the vegetables soften without browning, about 5 minutes. This process of slowly cooking vegetables without browning is called *sweating*.

5 **Simmer the fumet**
Add the fish heads and/or bones and the wine. Add water to cover the ingredients by about 1 inch (2.5 cm); more water could dilute the flavor of the finished fumet. Raise the heat to high. As soon as you see bubbles forming, reduce the heat to low. Skim off any foam from the surface of the fumet with a large slotted spoon or skimmer. The foam is the impurities being released from the bones; if not removed, it will cloud the fumet. Add the bouquet garni to the pot. Let the fumet simmer, regularly skimming any foam on the surface, until it is full flavored, about 35 minutes. Add additional water, if necessary, to keep the ingredients just submerged. Watch that the fumet doesn't come to a boil, or it will become cloudy, which will affect any sauces made from it.

6 **Strain the fumet**
Carefully pour the fumet through a sieve lined with damp cheesecloth into a large tempered glass or stainless-steel bowl and discard the solids. Because fish is much leaner than meat or poultry, the fumet will not need to be defatted like a meat or poultry stock. Use the fumet at once, or cool and store it.

7 **Cool and store the fumet**
Fill a large bowl partway with ice water and set the fumet in the ice bath to cool to room temperature, stirring occasionally. Cover and refrigerate for up to 2 days. Fumet is not a good candidate for freezing, as it easily picks up unwanted flavors. It's best to make it in small batches for use within a couple of days.

CHEF'S TIP
Fish markets, especially in Asian neighborhoods, are good sources for bones. Many customers buy whole fish and then ask the fishmongers to fillet them, so the markets often have a ready stock of fish heads and bones.

RECOMMENDED USES
In sauces for serving with fish, such as Herbed Sauce for Fish (page 67).

Companion Dishes for Sauces

Poached salmon with hollandaise sauce, grilled chicken with barbecue sauce—some combinations are classic. But whether you are using a sauce as a finishing touch or as a primary component of a dish, it must play a complementary role, neither overshadowing the other ingredients nor disappearing fully into them. The following are simple recipes for poached, panfried, roasted, and grilled foods that can be paired with the sauces in this book.

STEAMING

INGREDIENT	PREPARATION	TIMING & DONENESS
Broccoli florets, cauliflower florets, thick asparagus stalks, or green beans	Fill a saucepan with ½ inch (12 mm) of water and bring to a simmer. Add a collapsible metal steamer basket and arrange 1 layer of vegetables on top.	Cover the pan and steam until the vegetable is tender when pierced with the tip of a small knife, 4–6 minutes.

BOILING

INGREDIENT	PREPARATION	TIMING & DONENESS
New potatoes	Fill a large saucepan three-fourths full of water and bring to a boil. Add 1 tablespoon salt, then the potatoes.	Cook, uncovered, until tender when pierced with the tip of a small knife, 12–15 minutes.
Artichokes	Fill a large saucepan three-fourths full of water and bring to a boil. Add the trimmed artichokes.	Cook, uncovered, until tender when pierced in the stem with a small knife, about 40 minutes.

POACHING

INGREDIENT	PREPARATION	TIMING & DONENESS
Salmon fillets	Fill a frying pan with 2 inches (5 cm) of water, ½ cup (4 fl oz/125 ml) dry white wine, and 1 teaspoon salt and bring to a very low simmer. Add the fish.	Be sure the fish is submerged by 1 inch (2.5 cm) and cook until it flakes when prodded with a knife tip, about 10 minutes per inch of thickness.
Eggs, cracked into small custard cups	Fill a frying pan with 2 inches of water and bring to a very low simmer. Add 1 teaspoon vinegar, then pour in each egg.	Cook until the whites are set and the yolks are to your liking, 3 minutes for runny yolks and 5 minutes for set yolks.

PANFRYING

INGREDIENT	PREPARATION	TIMING & DONENESS
Thin white fish fillets or boneless chicken breasts	Dredge in seasoned flour. Pour a thin layer of oil in a frying pan over medium-high heat. When hot, add the food.	Cook until browned and the center is opaque, 1½–2 minutes per side for fish and 5–6 minutes per side for chicken.
Medallions of beef or lamb	Season with salt and pepper. Pour a thin layer of oil in a frying pan over medium-high heat. When hot, add the meat.	Cook until the browned and the center is done to your liking, 3 minutes per side for medium-rare.

INGREDIENT	PREPARATION	TIMING & DONENESS
Boneless beef roast, such as eye of round	Rub with oil and season well with salt and pepper. Place on a rack in a roasting pan, then put on the middle rack in a preheated 400°F (200°C) oven.	Cook until an instant-read thermometer inserted into the center reads 130°F (54°C) for medium-rare, about 15 minutes per pound. Let the meat rest for at least 10 minutes before carving.
Beef tenderloin	Rub with oil and season well with salt and pepper. Place on a rack in a roasting pan, then put on the middle rack in a preheated 400°F (200°C) oven.	Cook until an instant-read thermometer inserted into the center reads 130°F (54°C) for medium-rare, about 10 minutes per pound. Let the meat rest for at least 10 minutes before carving.
Pork tenderloin	Rub with oil and season well with salt and pepper. Place on a rack in a roasting pan, then put on the middle rack in a preheated 400°F (200°C) oven.	Cook until an instant-read thermometer inserted into the center reads 135°F (57°C) for medium. Let rest for at least 10 minutes before carving.
Whole poultry, such as chicken, game hen, or turkey	Rub with oil or melted butter and season well with salt and pepper. Place on a rack in a roasting pan, then put on the middle rack in a preheated 400°F (200°C) oven.	Cook until an instant-read thermometer inserted into the meaty part of the thigh, away from the bone, reads 170°F (77°C), 20–25 minutes per pound. Let rest for at least 10 minutes before carving.

INGREDIENT	PREPARATION	TIMING & DONENESS
Bone-in chicken breasts	Rub with oil, season well with salt and pepper, then place directly over hot coals or over the heat elements on a gas grill.	Cook until an instant-read thermometer inserted away from the bone reads 170°F (77°C), about 10 minutes per side.
Steaks, such as strip steak or ribeye	Rub with oil, season well with salt and pepper, then place directly over hot coals or over the heat elements of a gas grill.	Cook until an instant-read thermometer inserted away from the bone reads 130°F (54°C) for medium-rare, 2½–4 minutes per side.
Pork or veal chops	Rub with oil, season well with salt and pepper, then place directly over hot coals or over the heat elements of a gas grill.	Cook until an instant-read thermometer inserted away from the bone reads 135°F (54°C) for medium, 4–6 minutes per side.
Meaty fish steaks, such as tuna or salmon	Rub with oil, season well with salt and pepper, then place directly over hot coals or over the heat elements of a gas grill.	Cook until the fish is cooked to your liking, 3–5 minutes per side for medium-rare.

2

Key Techniques

Once you've mastered stock making, you'll be ready to learn other sauce-making skills, like deglazing, thickening, and emulsifying. You'll discover how to handle a number of typical sauce ingredients, too, including vegetables, herbs, and citrus juice and zest. You can turn back to this chapter whenever you encounter a confusing part of a recipe, or simply when you need a little extra help.

Dicing an Onion

1 Cut the onion in half
Using a chef's knife, cut the onion in half lengthwise, through the root end. This makes it easier to peel and gives each half a flat side for stability when making your cuts.

2 Peel the onion
Using a paring knife, pick up the edge of the onion's papery skin and pull it away. You may also need to remove the first layer of onion if it, too, has rough or papery patches.

3 Trim the onion
Trim each end neatly, leaving some of the root intact to help hold the onion half together. Place an onion half, flat side down, on a cutting board with the root end facing away from you.

4 Cut the onion lengthwise
Hold the onion securely on either side. Using a chef's knife, make a series of lengthwise cuts, as thick as you want the final dice to be. Do not cut all the way through the root end.

5 Cut the onion horizontally
Spread your fingers across the onion to help keep it together. Turn the knife blade parallel to the cutting board and make a series of horizontal cuts as thick as you want the final dice to be.

6 Cut the onion crosswise
Still holding the onion together with your fingers, cut it crosswise to make dice. Dicing an onion in this methodical way gives you pieces that cook evenly.

Dicing a Shallot

1 Separate the cloves

Sometimes you'll find plump, individual bronze-skinned shallots; other times they resemble garlic heads, with 2 or more cloves attached to one another. Separate the cloves.

2 Cut the shallot in half

When you are first learning to dice shallots, you may want to use a paring knife. As you gain skill, you can switch to a larger knife. Cut the shallot in half lengthwise, through the root end.

3 Peel and trim the shallot

Using the knife, pick up the edge of the shallot's papery skin and pull it away. Trim each end neatly, but leave some of the root intact to help hold the shallot half together.

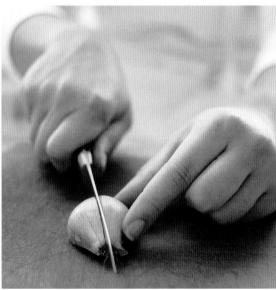
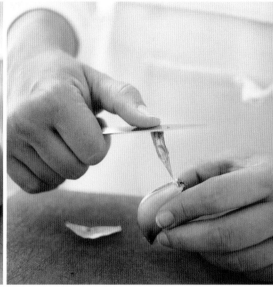

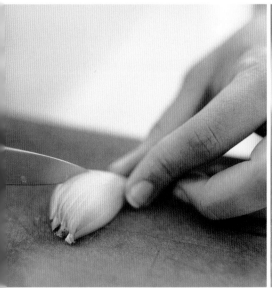

4 Cut the shallot lengthwise

Put the flat side of the shallot on the cutting board and make a series of thin lengthwise cuts. Do not cut all the way through the root end; it will hold the shallot layers together.

5 Cut the shallot horizontally

Turn the knife blade parallel to the cutting board and make a series of thin horizontal cuts.

6 Cut the shallot crosswise

Now, cut the shallot crosswise to make dice. Dicing a shallot in this methodical way gives pieces that cook evenly.

Dicing Carrots

TECHNIQUE

1 Trim the carrots
Start with good-quality, unblemished carrots. Use a vegetable peeler to remove the rough skin. Switch to a chef's knife and trim off the leafy tops and rootlike ends.

2 Cut the carrots into lengths
Cut the carrots into even lengths no longer than about 3 inches (7.5 cm). Shorter pieces are simpler to handle, making cutting and then dicing easier.

3 Create a flat surface
Before cutting each length of carrot, cut a thin slice from one side to create a flat surface. Turn the carrot piece onto this flat side to keep it stable while you cut.

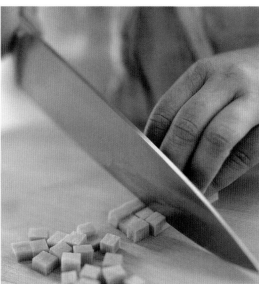

4 Cut the lengths into slices
Cut the carrot piece lengthwise into slices as thick as you want the final dice to be. (For example, if you are aiming for ¼-inch/6-mm dice, cut the carrot into ¼-inch-thick slices.)

5 Cut the slices into sticks
Stack 2 or 3 carrot slices and turn them so they are lying on their wide sides. Cut them lengthwise into sticks that are as thick as the first slices.

6 Cut the sticks into dice
Cut the carrot sticks crosswise to create dice. Dicing carrots methodically creates evenly sized pieces that cook at the same rate. Repeat with the remaining carrot lengths.

Dicing Celery

1 Trim the root end

Start with firm, unblemished celery with fresh-looking leaves. Using a chef's knife, trim the head of the celery as needed where the stalks meet the root end. Rinse the stalks.

2 Chop the leaves (optional)

The leaves are used in some dishes to provide extra celery flavor. Cut the leaves from the stalks and chop as directed in a recipe, usually coarsely.

TROUBLESHOOTING

Some celery today is string free, but you may still encounter stringy stalks. The outside ribs may also have a tough outer layer. To remove this layer or any strings, run a vegetable peeler over the stalk.

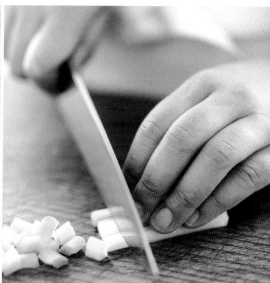

3 Cut the celery into lengths

Cut the celery stalks into even lengths no longer than about 3 inches (7.5 cm). Shorter pieces are simpler to handle, making slicing and then dicing easier.

4 Cut the lengths into sticks

Cut the celery pieces lengthwise into sticks as thick as you want the final dice to be. (For example, if you are aiming for ¼-inch/6-mm dice, cut the celery into ¼-inch-thick sticks.)

5 Cut the sticks into dice

Cut the celery sticks crosswise to create dice. Dicing celery methodically creates evenly sized pieces that cook at the same rate. Repeat with the remaining celery lengths.

Working with Garlic

1 Loosen the garlic peel
Using the flat side of a chef's knife, firmly press against the clove. If you plan to mince the garlic, it's fine to smash it. If you are slicing it, use light pressure to keep the clove intact.

2 Peel and halve the clove
The pressure from the knife will cause the garlic peel to split. Grasp the peel with your fingers, pull it away, then discard it. Cut the garlic clove in half lengthwise to make flat sides.

TROUBLESHOOTING

You may see a small green sprout running through the middle of a garlic clove. If left in, it could impart a bitter flavor to the dish. Use the tip of a paring knife to pop out the sprout, and then discard it.

3 Cut the garlic into slices
Working with one clove half at a time, use the knife to cut the garlic into very thin slices. Use the slices, or, if chopping or mincing, gather the slices in a pile in the center of the board.

4 Chop the garlic
Rest the fingertips of one hand on top of the tip of the knife. Move the heel of the knife in a rhythmic up-and-down motion over the garlic slices until evenly chopped.

5 Mince the garlic
Stop occasionally to clean the knife of garlic bits and gather them in a compact pile on the board. Continue to chop until the garlic pieces are very fine, or *minced*.

Zesting & Juicing Citrus

1 Zest the lemon
If you are zesting and juicing a lemon, zest it first. Use a rasp grater or the grating teeth on a box grater-shredder to remove only the colored part of the peel, not the bitter white pith.

2 Clean off the grater
Don't forget to scrape all the zest from the back of a grater, where some of it naturally gathers.

Seeding a Tomato

1 Halve the tomato
To seed a round or globe tomato, use a chef's knife to cut it in half through its "equator." If using a plum (Roma) tomato, cut it in half lengthwise.

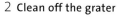

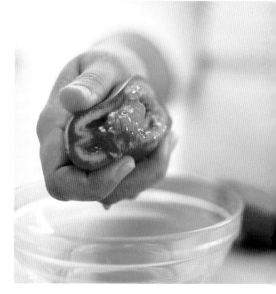

3 Cut the lemon in half
To juice a lemon, first press and roll it firmly against the counter to break some of the membranes holding in the juice. Then, using a chef's knife, cut the fruit in half crosswise.

4 Juice the lemon
To extract as much juice as possible, use a citrus reamer to pierce the membranes as you squeeze. Catch the juice in a bowl, and strain to remove seeds before using.

2 Squeeze and scoop out seeds
Gently squeeze the tomato half over a bowl. Use a finger, if necessary, to help scoop out the seed sacs (and any excess liquid). Tomatoes are seeded to give a sauce a smoother texture.

Peeling & Chopping Ginger

1 Peel the ginger

Using a vegetable peeler, peel away the papery brown skin to reveal the light, smooth flesh underneath.

2 Chop the ginger

Cut the peeled ginger into disks, and then cut the disks into strips. Cut the strips crosswise to create small pieces. If mincing, rock the knife over the ginger until the pieces are very fine.

Clarifying Butter

1 Melt the butter

Your goal is to separate the butterfat from the milk solids and excess liquid. Melt the butter in a saucepan over medium heat. After it melts, wait until the butter starts to bubble rapidly.

3 Pour off the butterfat

Carefully pour the clear yellow butterfat into a heatproof cup. Pour very slowly, avoiding the white milk solids and liquid that have settled on the bottom of the pan.

2 Evaporate the liquid and skim

Immediately reduce the heat to medium-low and cook for 1 minute. Turn off the burner or remove the pan from the heat, let stand for 2 minutes, and then skim off the foam.

4 Leave behind the milk products

Discard the white milk solids and the liquid. These are the part of butter that burns. Use the clarified butter as directed in a recipe.

Separating Eggs

1 Crack the egg

Eggs are easiest to separate when cold. Have 3 clean, grease-free bowls ready. To reduce shell fragments, crack the side of the egg sharply on a flat surface, rather than the rim of a bowl.

2 Pull apart the shell halves

Hold the cracked egg over an empty bowl and carefully pull the shell apart, letting the white (but not the yolk) start to drop into the bowl.

3 Pass the yolk back and forth

Transfer the yolk back and forth from one shell half to the other, letting the white fall away completely into the bowl below. Be careful not to break the yolk on a sharp shell edge.

4 Put the yolk in another bowl

Gently drop the yolk into the second bowl. Keeping the whites free of any yolk is key if you plan to whip the whites. A trace of yolk or other fat will prevent them from foaming.

TROUBLESHOOTING

If a yolk breaks as you separate the egg and gets into the white, this egg white cannot be used for whipping. Reserve the white for another use (like making scrambled eggs) or discard it. Rinse the bowl before continuing.

5 Put the white in another bowl

If the egg separates cleanly, pour the white into the third bowl. Break each new egg over the first empty bowl to avoid spoiling a batch of whites.

Thickening with a Slurry

1 Combine cornstarch and water
To make what chefs call a "slurry" for thickening pan sauces or reduction sauces, combine equal parts cornstarch (cornflour) and cold water or another liquid in a small bowl.

2 Stir the ingredients together
Using a fork, stir together the cornstarch and water until blended. The mixture should be the consistency of heavy (double) cream.

3 Bring the sauce base to a simmer
If needed, heat the sauce base until small bubbles appear. The slurry must be added to a hot liquid in order for it to thicken.

4 Add a small amount of slurry
If the slurry separates before you're ready to use it, stir again to combine. Drizzle a small amount of the slurry into the simmering sauce base. You may not need to use all of it.

5 Whisk the mixture
Whisk the slurry and liquid. Let the liquid come to a boil to activate the thickening power. If needed, whisk in more slurry a little at a time and cook until thickened as desired.

6 Check the consistency and flavor
A sauce thickened with a slurry has a glossy sheen. Taste it to make sure the chalky starch flavor has been cooked away. If not, simmer it briefly to remove the chalkiness.

Thickening with a Roux

TECHNIQUE

1 Heat the fat
A roux is a blend of fat and flour that thickens a sauce. The fat can be oil, butter, or rendered fat from a roast. If the fat is not already hot, heat it over medium to medium-high heat.

2 Add the flour
Once the fat is hot, sprinkle in the flour, following the proportions in the recipe and distributing it evenly over the bottom of the pan.

3 Whisk the flour with the fat
Using a whisk—preferably a flat roux whisk—stir the flour and fat until well combined. The flour will absorb the fat and may darken slightly.

4 Let the roux cook
After whisking, let the roux bubble for a minute or longer, as directed in the recipe. The longer it cooks, the darker and more flavorful it will be, but the less thickening power it will have.

5 Add heated liquid
After the roux has cooked to the stage directed in a recipe, stir in the liquid that will be thickened. The liquid should also be hot, to prevent dangerous spattering of hot fat.

6 Check the consistency and flavor
A sauce thickened with roux has an opaque appearance. Taste it to make sure the starchy flour flavor has been cooked away. If not, simmer it briefly to remove the starchiness.

Bouquet Garni

1 Wrap the ingredients
Bundling herbs and spices keeps them contained to ease skimming and straining. Rinse and wring out the cheesecloth (muslin), lay it on a work surface, and place the items on top.

2 Tie the bundle
Bring the corners of the cheesecloth together and tie with kitchen string, forming a secure bundle.

Working with Chiles

1 Quarter the chile
Many cooks wear a disposable latex glove on the hand that touches the chile to prevent irritation from its potent oils. Using a paring knife, cut the chile in half, then in quarters.

2 Remove the seeds and ribs
Cut away the seeds, ribs, and stem from each chile quarter. *Capsaicin*, the compound that makes chiles hot, is concentrated in these areas; removing them lessens the heat.

3 Cut the quarters into strips
Place the quarters, cut side up, on the cutting board. Cut into narrow slices about 1/8 inch (3 mm) thick. Take care not to pierce the glove.

4 Mince the strips
Line up the chile strips and cut them crosswise at 1/8-inch intervals. Rest your fingertips on the top of the tip of the knife and rock the heel of the knife over the pieces to mince them.

Deglazing

1 Add liquid to a hot pan

Place a pan containing the browned drippings left by a sauté or roast—called the *fond*—over medium-high heat until the drippings sizzle. Add stock or another liquid.

Mounting Sauces with Butter

1 Cut butter into small cubes

Keep the butter cold until you're ready to use it. Cut the butter in half lengthwise, then turn the slices 90 degrees and cut lengthwise again. Cut crosswise into small cubes.

2 Add the butter gradually

Remove the sauce from the heat or place it over low heat. Add one or a few cubes of butter at a time while whisking constantly.

2 Scrape up the browned bits

As the liquid comes to a boil, stir and scrape the bottom and sides of the pan with a wooden spatula to loosen the brown *fond*. It will be absorbed into the liquid for flavor and color.

3 Incorporate the butter

Keep whisking the sauce until the first addition of butter is completely incorporated, then add a little more. You don't want to let the butter just melt; instead, actively incorporate it.

4 Check the consistency

Mounting a sauce with butter increases its volume and gives it an appealing sheen and a smooth texture. It also thickens it slightly without the use of cornstarch (cornflour) or flour.

TECHNIQUE

Fixing a Broken Hollandaise Sauce

1 Pour the sauce into a cup
To repair the broken hollandaise, it needs to be slowly drizzled into fresh egg yolks. Start by pouring the sauce and any remaining butter into a liquid measuring cup.

2 Clean the bowl
Thoroughly wash and dry the bowl so you can make a fresh start with the hollandaise sauce.

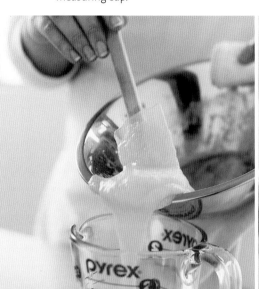

3 Start fresh with new yolks
Put 2 egg yolks into the clean bowl. Using an electric mixer, beat the yolks with 1 tablespoon water until thickened. Place over barely simmering water in a saucepan.

4 Drizzle in the broken sauce
While beating constantly with the mixer, drizzle the broken hollandaise into the egg yolks just a little at a time—more slowly than you added the butter the first time.

5 Check the consistency
By carefully controlling the rate at which you combine the broken sauce and the fresh yolks, you can re-emulsify a separated hollandaise. Taste and adjust the seasonings.

TROUBLESHOOTING

If you combine the oil and egg too quickly while making mayonnaise, the sauce may "break," or separate, developing a curdled appearance. It's relatively simple to bring back the sauce.

TECHNIQUE

Fixing a Broken Mayonnaise

1 Pour the sauce into a cup

To repair the broken mayonnaise, it needs to be slowly drizzled into a fresh egg yolk. Start by pouring the sauce and any remaining oil into a liquid measuring cup.

2 Clean the bowl

Thoroughly wash and dry the bowl so you can make a fresh start with the mayonnaise.

3 Start with a new yolk

Separate another egg and put the yolk into the clean bowl. Add 1 tablespoon of the broken sauce and beat together with an electric mixer.

4 Slowly add the broken sauce

While beating constantly with the mixer, gradually drizzle in the broken mayonnaise, adding it more slowly than you added the oil the first time.

5 Check the consistency

By carefully controlling the rate at which you combine the broken sauce and the fresh yolk, you can re-emulsify a separated mayonnaise. Taste and adjust the seasonings.

3

Pan Sauces & Reduction Sauces

This chapter embraces a wide variety of sauces, but they all start with a liquid that is simmered to reduce the volume and concentrate the flavor. Sometimes thickened with a slurry or a roux, these sauces often make use of the savory pan drippings left after cooking meat or poultry. As a bonus, you'll learn skills for panfrying and roasting that you can use to create other flavorful sauces.

Pan Sauce

This all-purpose pan sauce owes its light consistency to a simple technique: adding stock to the drippings in a frying pan (or roasting pan) and then simmering until barely thickened. Despite its light texture, the sauce carries a big flavor, so that only a few spoonfuls will dramatically enhance a dish.

1 Season the pork chops
Sprinkle the salt and pepper on both sides of the chops and set aside.

2 Select a pan
Select a heavy-bottomed 12-inch (30-cm) sauté pan with a lid. It should be large enough to hold the chops without crowding, as they need plenty of room to brown. You can use 2 pans if needed. A pan with an uncoated surface works best, but a nonstick pan will work, too. You want browned bits of meat to stick to the bottom of the pan to create what chefs call a *fond*, or base, for making the sauce.

3 Brown the pork chops
Place the pan over medium-high heat. Add the oil and heat until the surface just shimmers. Add the pork chops and cook until browned on the first side, about 2 minutes. Turn carefully and cook until browned on the second side, about 2 minutes longer. Reduce the heat to medium and cover the pan. Cook the chops for 3 minutes, then turn and cook on the other side until the chops are firm but not hard when pressed with a fingertip, about 3 minutes longer. The meat should be nicely browned. Transfer the chops to a platter and cover loosely with aluminum foil.

4 Evaluate the pan drippings
The directions that follow will work for the drippings from a roast in a roasting pan as well as those from chops in a sauté pan. Ideally, the drippings will be dark brown. If they are not, the final sauce will lack the color and flavor that comes with deep caramelization. This is usually more of an issue with roasted dishes than with panfried dishes. If necessary, darken the drippings by placing the pan over high heat—1 burner for a sauté pan, 2 burners for a roasting pan—and cook them for a few minutes until they are dark brown. >

For the pork chops

¼ teaspoon salt

⅛ teaspoon freshly ground pepper

4 bone-in center-cut pork chops, about ½ lb (250 g) each, patted dry, at room temperature

2 tablespoons canola oil

For the pan sauce

1½ cups (12 fl oz/375 ml) Brown Meat Stock (page 20) or Brown Poultry Stock (page 18)

1 tablespoon unsalted butter at room temperature, plus 2 tablespoons cold unsalted butter for finishing sauce

½ shallot, finely chopped

2 tablespoons water, optional

1½ teaspoons cornstarch (cornflour), optional

¼ teaspoon salt

¼ teaspoon freshly ground pepper

1 tablespoon chopped fresh sage, optional

MAKES ABOUT 1 CUP (8 FL OZ/250 ML)

RECOMMENDED USES
Substitute steak, chicken breasts, or lamb medallions for the pork chops, and add a complementary herb (page 51).

5 **Degrease the pan drippings**

Pour any juices from the pan into a 2-cup (16–fl oz/500-ml) degreasing cup or glass measuring cup. (Roasted foods usually create more drippings than stove-top cooking.) Let the drippings stand for a few minutes so that the fat separates from the juices. If you used a degreasing cup, pour off the juices into a glass measuring cup and discard the fat left behind. If you used a measuring cup, using a soupspoon, skim off and discard any clear fat that rises to the surface of the juices. Add enough stock to the degreased pan juices to make a total of 1½ cups (12 fl oz/375 ml).

6 **Cook the shallot**

Place the pan over high heat, again using 2 burners if using a roasting pan. Add the 1 tablespoon room-temperature butter and heat until the butter melts and the foam subsides and the browned bits in the bottom of the pan are sizzling. Add the shallot to the pan and cook, stirring, until the shallot softens and becomes translucent, about 1 minute.

7 **Deglaze the pan and reduce the liquid**

If you are not sure how to deglaze a pan, turn to page 41. Pour the stock into the pan and bring to a boil, scraping up the browned bits on the bottom and sides of the pan with a wooden spatula. These browned bits, or *fond*, will add good flavor to the final sauce. Once the liquid has absorbed the *fond*, let boil until the sauce is reduced to about 1 cup (8 fl oz/250 ml), about 3 minutes; the timing will depend on the size of the pan. Sauces like this one, made from a liquid reduced by evaporation during boiling, are sometimes called reduction sauces or reductions. Tilt the pan occasionally to estimate the amount of liquid remaining.

CHEF'S TIP

This recipe yields enough sauce for 4 servings, estimating ¼ cup (2 oz/60 ml) for each person. If you are serving more people, simply increase the amount of stock, reducing it by one-third of its volume, and proportionally increase the amount of dissolved cornstarch (if using) and butter.

8 Evaluate the consistency of the sauce

Tilt the pan and note the consistency of the sauce. If you feel it should be thicker, use a cornstarch slurry. Pour the water into a small bowl. Sprinkle the cornstarch over the water and stir to dissolve, making a slurry. Whisk a little of the slurry into the simmering sauce, then bring to a boil just until the sauce thickens, 1 minute or less. If the sauce is not sufficiently thickened, add a little more of the slurry and boil again. (For more details on using a slurry, turn to page 38.) If the sauce ends up too thick, thin it with additional stock or water, or any juices that have collected on the platter with the chops. If the sauce seems too thin, boil it for a minute or so to reduce it more.

8 >>

CHEF'S TIP

To heighten the flavor of a pan sauce, use a flavorful liquid such as stock or wine in place of water to make a slurry. Also, don't forget to add the juices that have collected on the platter while the meat or poultry was resting.

9 Mount the sauce with butter

Remove the pan from the heat. To find out more about mounting a sauce with butter, turn to page 41. Cut the cold butter into small cubes. Add the butter 1 cube at a time, moving an elongated whisk back and forth across the bottom of the pan until the butter is completely incorporated before adding the next cube. Mounting the finished sauce with butter gives the sauce a slightly thicker body and nice sheen.

10 Adjust the seasonings

Stir in the salt, pepper, and sage, if using, and taste the sauce; it should taste of the golden browned pork that was used to make it. If it is a little dull, add a bit more salt and or pepper until it tastes nicely balanced.

11 Serve the sauce

Place each pork chop on a warmed plate, and spoon a little sauce on top. Serve right away, passing any extra sauce in a small pitcher or sauceboat alongside.

Serving ideas

To illustrate how to make Pan Sauce, I have included instructions for panfrying pork chops in the master recipe and added sage to the sauce, but you can mix and match any kind of panfried or roasted poultry or meat with the appropriate stock and your favorite fresh herb. There are also countless ways to vary the flavors of a pan sauce, a handful of which are illustrated in the variations on pages 52–53.

Steak with parsley pan sauce (top left)
Flat-leaf (Italian) parsley has a crisp, fresh flavor that goes well with any meat or poultry—here, slices of tender beef.

Chicken breasts with tarragon pan sauce (left)
Tarragon, a delicately scented herb favored by French cooks, pairs nicely with mild chicken and fish. (More pronounced flavors would overpower tarragon.) This sauce is also nice with panfried veal medallions.

Lamb medallions with mint pan sauce (above)
Dainty medallions of tender, rich lamb are well matched with aromatic mint, which is a take on classic roast lamb with mint jelly.

Pan Sauce Variations

Made with just a base of stock, some aromatics and seasonings, and a nub of butter, Pan Sauce (page 47) is a good foundation for other flavorings. Mastering the making of it has taught you how to deglaze a pan, reduce a liquid, thicken a sauce with a slurry, and mount a sauce with butter, lessons that you can now apply to the variations that appear here. These sauces can be mixed and matched according to your taste with just about any meat or poultry that might come out of your frying or roasting pan. Just remember to use a meat stock for meat dishes and a poultry stock for poultry dishes.

White Wine Pan Sauce

Dry white wine provides a gently acidic layer of flavor. It's delicious paired with panfried chicken breasts.

Start with a panfry or roast. Degrease the pan juices, then add enough Brown Meat Stock (page 20) or Brown Poultry Stock (page 18) to make a total of 1 cup (8 fl oz/250 ml). Darken the pan drippings if necessary.

Place the frying pan or roasting pan over high heat and add 1 tablespoon room-temperature unsalted butter. When melted, add ½ finely chopped shallot to the pan and sauté until softened, about 1 minute. Add ½ cup (4 fl oz/125 ml) dry white wine such as Sauvignon Blanc or Pinot Grigio and reduce by half, about 1 minute. Deglaze with the pan juices and stock. Let boil until the sauce is reduced to about 1 cup (8 fl oz/250 ml), about 3 minutes.

If the sauce needs thickening, add a slurry of 2 tablespoons water and 1½ teaspoons cornstarch (cornflour) and bring to a boil until the desired thickness is reached. Remove the pan from the heat and whisk in 2 tablespoons cubed cold unsalted butter, a piece at a time, until thick and shiny. Adjust the seasonings and serve right away.

Madeira Pan Sauce

You can serve this full-flavored sauce with duck breasts or a thick rib-eye steak. If you wish, substitute dry sherry or tawny port for the Madeira.

Start with a panfry or roast. Degrease the pan juices, then add enough Brown Meat Stock (page 20) or Brown Poultry Stock (page 18) to make a total of 1¼ cups (10 fl oz/310 ml). Darken the pan drippings if necessary.

Place the frying pan or roasting pan over high heat and add 1 tablespoon room-temperature unsalted butter. When melted add ½ finely chopped shallot to the pan and sauté until softened, about 1 minute. Add ¼ cup (2 fl oz/60 ml) Madeira and reduce by half, about 30 seconds. Deglaze with the pan juices and stock. Let boil until the sauce is reduced to about 1 cup (8 fl oz/250 ml), about 3 minutes.

If the sauce needs thickening, add a slurry of 2 tablespoons water and 1½ teaspoons cornstarch (cornflour) and bring to a boil until the desired thickness is reached. Remove the pan from the heat and whisk in 2 tablespoons cubed cold unsalted butter, a piece at a time, until thick and shiny. Adjust the seasonings and serve right away.

Herbed Cream Pan Sauce

This sauce is an excellent match with chicken, pork, or veal.

Start with a panfry or roast. Degrease the pan juices, then add enough Brown Meat Stock (page 20) or Brown Poultry Stock (page 18) to make a total of 1¼ cups (10 fl oz/310 ml). Darken the pan drippings if necessary.

Place the frying pan or roasting pan over high heat, and add 1 tablespoon room-temperature unsalted butter. When melted, add ½ finely chopped shallot to the pan and sauté until softened, about 1 minute. Add ¼ cup (2 fl oz/60 ml) heavy (double) cream and 1 tablespoon chopped fresh flat-leaf (Italian) parsley or chives and reduce by half, about 30 seconds. Deglaze with the pan juices and stock. Let boil until the sauce is reduced to about 1 cup (8 fl oz/250 ml), about 3 minutes.

If the sauce needs thickening, add a slurry of 2 tablespoons water and 1½ teaspoons cornstarch (cornflour) and bring to a boil until the desired thickness is reached. Remove the pan from the heat and whisk in 2 tablespoons cubed cold unsalted butter, a piece at a time, until thick and shiny. Adjust the seasonings and serve right away.

Mustard Pan Sauce

Flavored mustards, such as those laced with herbs, can stand in for the Dijon mustard. Serve the sauce with panfried chicken breasts.

Start with a panfry or roast. Degrease the pan juices, then add enough Brown Meat Stock (page 20) or Brown Poultry Stock (page 18) to make a total of 1½ cups (12 fl oz/375 ml). Darken the pan drippings if necessary.

Place the frying pan or roasting pan over high heat and add 1 tablespoon room-temperature unsalted butter. When melted, add ½ finely chopped shallot to the pan and sauté until softened, about 1 minute. Deglaze with the pan juices and stock. Let boil until the sauce is reduced to about 1 cup (8 fl oz/250 ml), about 3 minutes.

If the sauce needs thickening, add a slurry of 2 tablespoons water and 1½ teaspoons cornstarch (cornflour) and bring to a boil until the desired thickness is reached. Remove the pan from the heat and whisk in 2 tablespoons cubed cold unsalted butter, a piece at a time, until thick and shiny. Stir in 1½ tablespoons Dijon mustard. Adjust the seasonings and serve right away.

CHEF'S TIP

When making a pan sauce, poultry stock can be used for dishes made with poultry, but for the most savory sauce to accompany meat dishes such as beef or even venison, use beef- or veal-based meat stock. Pork has a neutral flavor that works with either stock.

Green Peppercorn Pan Sauce

Make this sauce to accompany beef tenderloin, either roasted whole or sliced into filets mignons and panfried.

Start with a panfry or roast. Degrease the pan juices, then add enough Brown Meat Stock (page 20) or Brown Poultry Stock (page 18) to make a total of 1¼ cups (10 fl oz/310 ml). Darken the pan drippings if necessary.

Place the frying pan or roasting pan over high heat and add 1 tablespoon room-temperature unsalted butter. When melted, add ½ finely chopped shallot to the pan and sauté until softened, about 1 minute. Add ¼ cup (2 fl oz/60 ml) heavy (double) cream and 2 tablespoons drained and rinsed brine-packed green peppercorns and reduce by half, about 30 seconds. Deglaze with the pan juices and stock. Let boil until the sauce is reduced to about 1 cup (8 fl oz/250 ml), about 3 minutes.

If the sauce needs thickening, add a slurry of 2 tablespoons water and 1½ teaspoons cornstarch (cornflour) and bring to a boil until the desired thickness is reached. Remove the pan from the heat and whisk in 2 tablespoons cubed cold unsalted butter, a piece at a time, until thick and shiny. Adjust the seasonings and serve right away.

Bourbon Pan Sauce

You must flame the bourbon to remove the raw alcohol flavor. This sauce is excellent with steak.

Start with a panfry or roast. Degrease the pan juices, then add enough Brown Meat Stock (page 20) or Brown Poultry Stock (page 18) to make a total of 1½ cups (12 fl oz/375ml). Darken the pan drippings if necessary.

Pour ⅓ cup (3 fl oz/80 ml) bourbon into a small saucepan and place over low heat until hot; do not allow to boil. Remove from the heat. Have a lid ready to extinguish the flame. Using a long match and averting your face, ignite the bourbon by holding the lit match just above the surface of the warmed liquid. Be careful of long hair and loose sleeves! Let flame for 30 seconds. Cover the saucepan with the lid to extinguish the flame. Add the flamed bourbon to the stock and juices.

Place the frying pan or roasting pan over high heat, and add 1 tablespoon room-temperature unsalted butter. When melted, add ½ finely chopped shallot to the pan and sauté until softened, about 1 minute. Deglaze with the pan juices, stock, and bourbon. Let boil until the sauce is reduced to about 1 cup (8 fl oz/250 ml), about 3 minutes.

If the sauce needs thickening, add a slurry of 2 tablespoons water and 1½ teaspoons cornstarch (cornflour) and bring to a boil until the desired thickness is reached. Remove the pan from the heat and whisk in 2 tablespoons cubed cold unsalted butter, a piece at a time, until thick and shiny. Adjust the seasonings and serve right away.

Pan Gravy

Pan gravy uses flour as a thickener. The flour is combined with fat to make a roux, which gives gravy a thicker texture and more opaque appearance than pan sauce. For the deepest flavor, the roux is made with the fat from the pan drippings after roasting foods, then the food and the gravy are served together.

1 Preheat the oven and select a pan

Preheat the oven to 400°F (200°C). Using high heat for roasting chicken makes the skin brown and crisp and contributes to a flavorful sauce. Select a roasting pan that fits the chicken well. The bird should not be crowded in the pan; you want the hot air of the oven to circulate freely around it. Nor do you want an overly large roasting pan, since you want to keep the drippings from burning on the pan bottom or evaporating. A roasting pan with an uncoated surface works best, but a nonstick pan will also work. You want browned bits of meat to stick to the bottom of the pan to create what chefs call a *fond*, or base, for making the gravy. And lastly, since you will use the roasting pan on the stove top when you make the gravy, make sure the pan is flameproof.

2 Prepare the chicken

Remove the giblets from the chicken cavity and reserve for another use or discard. Using paper towels, thoroughly pat dry the chicken. Rub the outside of the chicken with the softened butter and season the bird inside and out with the salt and pepper. Put the onion and rosemary inside the chicken's cavity. If desired, truss the chicken for a neat appearance, tying the legs together with kitchen string, and tuck the wing tips under the back.

3 Roast the chicken

Place the chicken on its side on an oiled V-shaped rack in the roasting pan. If necessary, prop the chicken in place using a crumpled piece of aluminum foil. Roast for 30 minutes. Turn the chicken on its other side and roast for 30 minutes longer. Turn the chicken on its back. Roast until an instant-read thermometer inserted into the thickest part of a thigh registers 170°F (77°C), about 45 minutes longer, for a total roasting time of about 1¾ hours. Slip a wooden spoon into the cavity, then tip the chicken so the juices run into the pan. Transfer the chicken to a warmed platter. Let the chicken rest for 10–15 minutes while you make the gravy. Resting will allow the juices to redistribute evenly throughout the bird.

4 Evaluate the pan drippings

The drippings in the pan used to make gravy should be dark brown. If not, the final gravy will lack the color and flavor that comes with deep caramelization. The drippings are often underbrowned with roasted foods. If necessary, darken the drippings by placing the pan over high heat—using 2 burners if necessary—and cook them for a few minutes until they are dark brown. >

For the roast chicken

1 roasting chicken, 6½ lb (3.25 kg)

2 tablespoons unsalted butter, at room temperature

½ teaspoon salt

¼ teaspoon freshly ground pepper

1 small yellow onion, peeled and quartered

2 sprigs fresh rosemary or thyme

For the pan gravy

About 1½ cups (16 fl oz/500 ml) Brown Poultry Stock (page 18)

About 2 tablespoons melted unsalted butter

3 tablespoons all-purpose (plain) flour

¼ teaspoon salt

¼ teaspoon freshly ground pepper

MAKES ABOUT 2 CUPS (16 FL OZ/500 ML)

CHEF'S TIP

You can increase or reduce the yield of this recipe by using this formula: For every 1 cup (8 fl oz/250 ml) liquid (juices plus stock), use 1½ tablespoons each fat and flour to make the roux. Using these proportions, you can make just the amount of gravy you need. Plan on about ½ cup (4 fl oz/125ml) gravy for each serving.

A degreasing cup is particularly handy when making pan sauces. The pan juices settle to the bottom of the cup and are easily poured off through the cup's long, slender spout, leaving the fat behind in the cup.

A flat roux whisk does a terrific job of making roux in the roasting pan or a frying pan. Its flat, angled shape allows it to reach into the corners of a roasting pan much better than other types of whisks.

5 Separate the fat from the pan juices

Pour any drippings from the pan into a 2-cup (16–fl oz/500-ml) degreasing cup or glass measuring cup. Let stand for a few minutes so the fat separates. If you used a degreasing cup, pour off the light brown pan juices into a 2-cup glass measuring cup; reserve the fat in the degreasing cup. If you used a measuring cup, using a soupspoon, skim off and reserve any clear yellow fat that rises to the surface of the drippings. Measure out 3 tablespoons of the reserved fat.

6 Supplement the fat and pan juices if needed

You're aiming for 2 cups (16 fl oz/500 ml) juices and 3 tablespoons fat. If needed, add enough stock to the degreased pan juices to make up the full amount; add melted butter to the fat to make up the full amount. If the stock is cold, use a small saucepan over medium heat to heat it up before using. Don't skimp on the amount of fat needed; it will be used to make a roux, and using the correct proportion of fat and flour is important to the flavor and texture of the final gravy. Too little fat and the roux will not develop a smooth, moist consistency or have a nice sheen, but will instead be hard and dry. The final result will be a gravy that lacks the rich, full flavor that everyone expects when a full sauceboat is placed on the table.

7 Make the roux

If you are not sure how to make a roux, turn to page 39. This mixture of fat and flour will thicken the gravy. Place the roasting pan over 2 burners on medium heat. Add the fat to the pan. When the fat is hot, sprinkle in the flour. Using a whisk—preferably a flat roux whisk—whisk the fat and flour until smooth. Let the roux bubble for 1 minute. It will look very brown, more from absorbing the color of the drippings than from cooking. The flour in roux loses its thickening power the longer it cooks, so cook the roux only for a minute or so. Any remaining raw flour flavor will be cooked out while the gravy simmers.

8 Cool the roux

Remove the pan from the heat and let the roux cool until it stops bubbling, about 1 minute. This will help prevent spattering when you add the liquid to the hot roux, as will heating the liquid before adding it. ›

> **CHEF'S TIP**
> *During the holidays, make turkey stock instead of chicken stock for a delicious turkey gravy. Use Brown Poultry Stock on page 18 as your base recipe, substituting turkey backs and wings for the chicken parts.*

9 **Add the stock and reduce the liquid**
Return the pan to medium-high heat on 2 burners. When the roux sizzles, whisk in the combined stock and pan juices and bring to a boil, scraping up the browned roux and drippings on the bottom and sides of the pan with the whisk. Reduce the heat to medium-low. Simmer the gravy, whisking often, until it has thickened to the consistency of heavy (double) cream. This will take about 10 minutes, depending on the size of the pan. The larger the pan, the more quickly the liquid will evaporate and reduce.

10 **Evaluate the consistency of the gravy**
The gravy should be thick enough to coat the back of a wooden spoon. To test, draw your finger through the gravy down the back of the spoon; it should leave a clear path. If the gravy is too thick, thin it with more heated stock or water. If too thin, continue to simmer until it reduces more and thickens.

11 **Adjust the seasonings and strain the gravy**
Stir in the salt and pepper and taste the gravy; it should taste rich but have a clear chicken flavor. If it tastes a little dull, stir in more salt or pepper until it tastes nicely balanced. Pour the gravy into a saucepan. If desired, strain it through a fine-mesh sieve as you do so, to remove any undissolved pan drippings. Keep warm over very low heat.

12 **Carve the chicken**
Fill a large sauceboat with hot tap water and let stand to warm while you carve the chicken. Using a sharp carving knife and a meat fork, carve the chicken. First, remove the legs: Cut through the skin between the leg and the breast to locate the thigh joint, then cut through the joint to remove the entire leg. Cut through the joint that separates the drumstick from the thigh. Repeat with the other leg. Next, remove the wings: Cut through the skin between the wing and breast to locate the shoulder joint, and cut through the joint to remove the wing. Repeat with the other wing. Finally, carve the breast: Just above the thigh and wing joints, carve a deep horizontal cut through the breast toward the bone, creating a base cut. Starting near the breastbone, carve thin slices vertically, cutting downward to end each slice at the base cut.

13 **Serve the gravy**
Pour out the water from the sauceboat and dry the sauceboat. Pour the gravy into the warmed sauceboat. Arrange the carved chicken on a platter or individual plates and serve, passing the gravy alongside. Serve right away.

Serving ideas

Gravy transforms a plain roasted bird into an irresistible treat. Don't save it just for the holidays. Instead, make the most of any food you roast by using the pan drippings to make gravy. To make gravy for roast beef or another meaty roast, use Brown Meat Stock (page 20) instead of the poultry stock. A little gravy goes a long way: rather than letting your food swim in sauce, spoon or pour it judiciously over the food.

Gravy spooned over poultry (top left)
An alternative to passing gravy in a sauceboat is to spoon the gravy over the sliced bird, letting it pool slightly on the sides. Follow the directions (opposite) for carving the chicken, then cut slices of the thigh and leg meat off the bone before plating.

Open-faced sandwich with gravy (left)
Leftover poultry and gravy make for a hearty second meal. Toast a slice of bread, tear the meat into bite-sized pieces, and pour warmed gravy over the top.

Mashed potatoes and gravy (above)
For many people, no meal with gravy is complete without mashed potatoes. Use the back of a spoon to make nooks and crannies to trap the gravy.

Béchamel Sauce

Béchamel is the most basic white sauce of all. Classically trained cooks are taught to make béchamel in three thicknesses. Thin béchamel can be used as the base of a soup, while thick béchamel is a requirement for soufflés. The medium-thick version has the most uses in a contemporary kitchen, and it is the sauce made here.

1 Cut a slice from the onion
Using a chef's knife, cut the onion in half lengthwise and peel it. Place the peeled half, flat side down, on the cutting board. Holding the knife blade parallel to the cutting board, cut a slice ¼ inch (6 mm) thick from the flat side. Set the slice aside to use for the sauce. Reserve the uncut onion half and the remainder of the cut onion half for another use.

2 Steep the onion and bay leaf in the milk
Although béchamel should have a neutral flavor, steeping an onion slice and a bay leaf in the milk lends a lovely fragrance and subtle flavor to the finished sauce. In a small saucepan, combine the milk, onion slice, and bay leaf. Place the pan over medium heat and heat just until tiny bubbles appear around the edge of the pan, about 5 minutes. Heating the mixture helps transfer the aromatic flavors of the onion and bay to the milk. Don't let the milk come to a boil; this causes a skin to form and will affect the texture of the sauce. Remove the saucepan from the heat, cover, and let stand for 10 minutes to infuse the milk with the flavor of the onion and bay leaf. Using a slotted spoon, remove and discard the onion and bay leaf. Re-cover to keep warm.

3 Select a saucepan
You will need a 2½- to 3-qt (2.5- to 3-l) heavy-bottomed saucepan for making the sauce. Although it will hold considerably more sauce than the recipe yields, you will appreciate the extra room when you are vigorously whisking the ingredients together. You can use any pan with straight sides, but a pan with sloped sides will allow you to dislodge more easily any flour that collects at the edge. If flour clings to the pan it can scorch, and the resulting sauce will have a burned flavor. >

---

1 small yellow onion

2 cups (16 fl oz/500 ml) whole milk

½ bay leaf

3 tablespoons unsalted butter, plus
1 tablespoon cold unsalted butter if you plan to hold the sauce

3 tablespoons all-purpose (plain) flour

¼ teaspoon salt

⅛ teaspoon freshly ground pepper, preferably white pepper

MAKES ABOUT 2 CUPS (16 FL OZ/500 ML)

 CHEF'S TIP
Many chefs favor white pepper over black pepper in light-colored sauces. White pepper is slightly milder than black pepper, and its pale color doesn't give the sauce a speckled appearance the way black pepper does.

> **RECOMMENDED USES**
> *As an ingredient in baked dishes, such as lasagna, or as a base for cheese sauces for cauliflower or broccoli gratins.*

4 Make the roux

To find out more about how to make a roux, turn to page 39. Add the 3 tablespoons butter to the pan and place it over medium-low heat. When the butter has melted, sprinkle in the flour and whisk to combine (a flat roux whisk works best for this, but you can also use a traditional whisk). Reduce the heat to low. Let the roux froth and bubble for 2 minutes. To keep the color of the final sauce a pale ivory, don't allow the roux to brown past pale beige; this is called a blond roux. (This is a short cooking time for roux, not long enough to cook off the flour, but the simmering in the next step will remove any remaining floury taste.) Remove the saucepan from the heat and let the roux cool until it stops bubbling, about 1 minute.

5 Simmer the sauce

Slowly and evenly whisk the warm milk into the roux, moving the whisk in a back-and-forth motion across the bottom of the pan. Return the mixture to the stove and bring to a boil over medium heat, whisking often. Reduce the heat to medium-low and simmer gently, whisking often, until the sauce thickens, about 5 minutes. You don't want to stray far from the stove during this process, as the sauce can easily burn if left unattended.

6 Evaluate the flavor and consistency

At this point, taste the sauce; if a raw flour taste remains, continue to simmer a little longer. To test the consistency of the sauce, dip a wooden spoon in the sauce to coat it. Draw your finger through the sauce down the middle of the back of the spoon: a bare track should remain without the sauce starting to fill it in. If you are using the sauce plain in a recipe, such as in lasagna, stir in the salt and pepper. If you are making a cheese sauce, do not season the sauce until after you add the cheese and taste the sauce, as the cheese itself will be salty.

7 Adjust the seasonings

Taste the sauce; it should taste creamy and fairly neutral, with a faint trace of onion and bay. Stir in a touch more salt or pepper if the sauce tastes dull.

8 Serve or hold the sauce

Use the sauce right away, or hold it. To hold the sauce for up to 2 hours, cut the 1 tablespoon cold butter into very small cubes and dot it over the surface of the sauce. As the butter melts, it will prevent a skin from forming on the surface. To store the sauce for up to 1 day, transfer the hot sauce to a storage container with a lid and dot with the butter. Press a piece of plastic wrap or waxed paper directly onto the surface of the sauce. Let the sauce cool completely, then cover with the lid and refrigerate. To use, reheat very slowly over low heat, stirring often.

Béchamel Sauce Variations

Making a good pale roux is the key to a creamy, subtle Béchamel Sauce (page 61) and is also the starting point for a variety of cheese sauces. Full-flavored aged cheeses will result in the most flavorful sauces. The classic Mornay sauce features two nutty-flavored cheeses, one Swiss and one Italian: Gruyère and Parmesan. To make a sauce featuring Italy's classic blue cheese, Gorgonzola, choose an aged "mountain" (*naturale*) Gorgonzola, which is sharper and firmer than Gorgonzola *dolce* or *dolcelatte*. Pass over mild Cheddar in favor of a sharp, aged farmstead Cheddar for making sauce. In each case, cook the sauce just long enough to melt the cheese, or the result will be gritty.

Mornay Sauce

Use this sauce for making a cauliflower or broccoli gratin.

Follow the recipe to make the béchamel. After evaluating the consistency of the sauce in step 6, whisk ½ cup (2 oz/60 g) shredded Gruyère cheese and 3 tablespoons freshly grated Parmigiano-Reggiano cheese into the sauce. Cook, whisking almost constantly, just until the cheeses have melted and the sauce is smooth.

Adjust the seasonings, keeping in mind that the cheeses themselves are salty, before using.

MAKES ABOUT 2 CUPS (16 FL OZ/500 ML)

Cheddar Sauce

Spoon this sauce over steamed or boiled vegetables, such as broccoli or potatoes, or use to make macaroni and cheese.

Follow the recipe to make the béchamel. After evaluating the consistency of the sauce in step 6, whisk 2 cups (8 oz/250 g) shredded extra-sharp Cheddar cheese into the sauce. Cook, whisking almost constantly, just until the cheese has melted and the sauce is smooth. Season the sauce using red hot-pepper sauce in place of freshly ground pepper.

Adjust the seasonings, keeping in mind that the cheese itself is salty, before using.

MAKES ABOUT 2⅓ CUPS (19 FL OZ/590 ML)

Gorgonzola Sauce

Rich, flavorful, and pungent, this sauce goes well with grilled steaks and roasted beef tenderloin.

Follow the recipe to make the béchamel. After evaluating the consistency of the sauce in step 6, whisk ⅔ cup (4 oz/125 g) crumbled Gorgonzola cheese into the sauce. Cook, whisking almost constantly, just until the cheese has melted and the sauce is smooth.

Adjust the seasonings, keeping in mind that the cheese itself is salty, before using.

MAKES ABOUT 2 CUPS (16 FL OZ/500 ML)

Velouté Sauce

Velouté means "velvety." At its best, this sauce should deliver on its name, with a light, silky texture and a somewhat translucent sheen. Although both are considered roux-based white sauces, velouté is much lighter in texture than its cousin béchamel because of the use of stock, rather than milk.

For the white stock

4 sprigs fresh flat-leaf (Italian) parsley

1 sprig fresh thyme

1 bay leaf

8 whole peppercorns

3 lb (1.5 kg) veal soup bones or marrowbones

2 lb (1 kg) chicken wings or backs, or a combination

1 large yellow onion, coarsely chopped

1 large carrot, coarsely chopped

1 large stalk celery with leaves, coarsely chopped

Pinch of salt

4 tablespoons (4 oz/125 g) unsalted butter, plus 1 tablespoon cold unsalted butter if you plan to hold the sauce

¼ cup (1½ oz/45 g) all-purpose (plain) flour

¼ cup (2 fl oz/60 ml) heavy (double) cream

¼ teaspoon salt

⅛ teaspoon freshly ground pepper, preferably white pepper

MAKES ABOUT 2 CUPS (16 FL OZ/500 ML)

RECOMMENDED USES
As an ingredient in classic French dishes or the base for flavored sauces made with fish, meat, or poultry stock (see variations, page 67).

1 **Prepare the ingredients for the stock**
If you are new to making white stock, turn to page 22. Up to 3 days in advance of making the sauce, prepare the stock. Wrap the parsley, thyme, bay leaf, and peppercorns in a damp piece of cheesecloth (muslin) and secure with kitchen string.

2 **Put the stock ingredients in a pot**
Combine the veal bones, chicken parts, onion, carrot, celery, and bouquet garni in a stockpot or large saucepan. Add water to cover the ingredients by about 1 inch (2.5 cm); more water could dilute the flavor of the finished stock. Bring just to a boil over high heat.

3 **Simmer the stock**
As soon as you see bubbles forming, reduce the heat to low. Skim off any foam from the surface of the stock with a large slotted spoon or skimmer. Simmer the stock, uncovered, regularly skimming any foam on the surface, until it is full flavored, at least 4 hours and up to 8 hours. Add hot water as needed to keep the ingredients just submerged. Never allow the stock to come to a boil, or fat from the meat will be suspended in the stock, giving the stock a greasy mouthfeel. To judge the flavor of the stock, ladle a bit of it into a cup. Stir in the salt and taste for a full, rounded flavor.

4 **Strain the stock**
Line a sieve with damp cheesecloth and place it over a large bowl. Carefully pour the stock through the sieve and discard the solids. Let the stock stand for 5 minutes to allow the fat to rise to the surface.

5 **Defat the stock**
Use a large metal spoon to skim the clear yellow fat from the surface of the strained stock. Or, if time allows, refrigerate the stock before defatting. Fill a large bowl partway with ice water and set the bowl of stock in the ice bath to cool to room temperature, stirring occasionally. Cover and refrigerate the stock overnight. The fat will rise to the top and solidify, making it easy to scrape it off the surface. Melt the gelatinous chilled stock over low heat before measuring it out.

6 **Measure out the stock**
Measure out 3 cups (24 fl oz/750 ml) of the stock and save the rest for another purpose. (Cover the stock and refrigerate for up to 3 days, or pour into airtight containers and freeze for up to 3 months.) ›

7 **Make the roux**
To find out more about how to make a roux, turn to page 39. Put the stock in a saucepan over medium heat. You will be adding it to a hot roux, and heating the stock first keeps the roux from splattering, which is what happens when a cold liquid is added. In a heavy-bottomed saucepan over medium-low heat, melt 4 tablespoons (2 oz/60 g) of the butter. Sprinkle in the flour. Using a whisk—preferably a flat roux whisk—whisk the butter and flour until smooth. Reduce the heat to low. Let the roux froth and bubble for 2 minutes. It may deepen slightly in color to a light beige. Don't worry if this happens, but to keep the color of the final sauce ivory don't let it get any darker. (This is called a blond roux.) Remove the pan from the heat and let the roux cool until it stops bubbling, about 1 minute.

8 **Simmer the sauce**
Slowly and evenly whisk the hot stock into the roux, moving the whisk in a back-and-forth motion across the bottom of the pan. Return the mixture to the stove and bring to a boil over medium heat, whisking often. Reduce the heat to very low. Move the saucepan to one side of the burner. (This directs the heat to one area of the saucepan and causes the foam to collect in that area, which makes the sauce easier to skim.) Cook the sauce, uncovered and at a low simmer, occasionally skimming off the white froth and film that forms on the surface with a large metal spoon, until it has reduced to a scant 2 cups (16 fl oz/500 ml), about 40 minutes. Don't leave the sauce unattended for too long, as it could easily burn if not tended to regularly. Remove the sauce from the heat and whisk in the cream, salt, and pepper. (A touch of cream lends richness to the sauce.)

9 **Adjust the seasonings and strain the sauce**
Taste the sauce; it should taste of the stock used to make it, with no trace of raw flour. If it tastes bland, stir in a small amount of salt and pepper until it tastes nicely balanced. If you wish, strain the sauce through a fine-mesh sieve to remove any remaining froth and film. (For an especially smooth texture, use a conical strainer, or *chinois*.)

10 **Use or hold the sauce**
Use the sauce right away, or hold it. To hold the sauce for up to 2 hours, cut the 1 tablespoon cold butter into very small cubes and dot it over the surface of the sauce. As the butter melts, it will prevent a skin from forming on the surface. To store the sauce for up to 1 day, transfer the hot sauce to a storage container with a lid and dot with the butter. Press a piece of plastic wrap or waxed paper directly onto the surface of the sauce. Let cool completely, then cover with the lid and refrigerate. To use, reheat very slowly over low heat, stirring often.

Velouté Sauce Variations

Once you have made Velouté Sauce (page 64) successfully, you will feel confident using two primary sauce-making techniques: making a roux and slowly reducing liquid to a good sauce consistency. This basic sauce is traditionally used for coquilles St.-Jacques and a handful of other dishes, but with a few simple adjustments, you can make three additional sauces. The first one uses a meat stock and a *mirepoix* (the French culinary trinity of onion, carrot, and celery), the second calls for fish fumet and summery fresh herbs, and the third marries poultry stock and *duxelles* (sautéed mushrooms and shallot, another French classic).

Modern Brown Sauce

This is a faster version of classic, labor-intensive French brown sauce. Serve with meat dishes.

In a heavy-bottomed saucepan over medium-low heat, melt 1 tablespoon unsalted butter. Add ½ cup (2½ oz/75 g) finely diced yellow onion, ¼ cup (1¼ oz/37 g) finely diced carrot, and ¼ cup (1¼ oz/37 g) finely diced celery and sauté until the vegetables are lightly browned, about 10 minutes. Transfer to a bowl and set aside.

Add 4 tablespoons (2 oz/60 g) unsalted butter to the pan. When melted, whisk in ⅓ cup (2 oz/60 g) all-purpose (plain) flour. Cook, whisking constantly, until the roux smells toasted and is a light walnut brown, about 8 minutes. Let cool slightly, then whisk in 4 cups (32 fl oz/1 l) warmed Brown Meat Stock (page 20). Add ¼ cup (2 fl oz/60 ml) Madeira, 1 teaspoon tomato paste, 2 sprigs fresh thyme, 3 sprigs fresh flat-leaf (Italian) parsley, and the reserved vegetables, whisking well. Bring to a boil, reduce the heat to a low simmer, and cook until the sauce is reduced to about 2 cups (16 fl oz/500 ml), about 40 minutes. Adjust the seasonings, strain, and serve or hold the sauce.

Herbed Sauce for Fish

Use this sauce in baked dishes with fish fillets or other seafood.

In a heavy-bottomed saucepan over medium-low heat, melt 4 tablespoons (2 oz/60 g) unsalted butter. Whisk in ¼ cup (1½ oz/45 g) all-purpose (plain) flour and cook over low heat, whisking constantly, until the roux is light beige, about 2 minutes. Let cool slightly, then whisk in 3 cups (24 fl oz/750 ml) warmed Fish Fumet (page 24). Bring to a boil, reduce the heat to a low simmer, and cook until the sauce is reduced to about 2 cups (16 fl oz/500 ml), about 40 minutes. Adjust the seasonings, strain, and pour into a clean saucepan.

Before serving, stir in 2 teaspoons minced fresh flat-leaf (Italian) parsley, 2 teaspoons minced fresh tarragon, and 2 teaspoons minced fresh chives and simmer for about 5 minutes to blend the flavors.

Shiitake Mushroom Sauce

With its earthy flavor and meaty texture, this versatile sauce is especially good in baked pork or chicken dishes.

Follow the recipe for Velouté Sauce, but substitute Brown Poultry Stock (page 18) for the White Stock.

While the sauce is simmering in step 8, coarsely chop the caps from 10 oz (315 g) fresh shiitake mushrooms (discard the stems). Place the caps in a food processor and pulse until finely chopped. Next, place a frying pan over medium heat and melt 2 tablespoons unsalted butter. When the foam subsides, add 1 large minced shallot and sauté until softened, about 2 minutes. Stir in the mushrooms and cook, stirring often, until the mushroom juices are completely evaporated and the mushrooms are tender and dry, about 12 minutes.

Stir the mushrooms into the reduced sauce. Simmer for about 5 minutes to blend the flavors, then adjust the seasonings and serve or hold the sauce (you won't need to strain it).

Kansas City–Style Barbecue Sauce

The basic ingredients of nearly every barbecue sauce are tomatoes, sugar, and vinegar, enhanced with chiles, herbs, spices, and other seasonings. While every area has its own recipe, Kansas City sets the standard with its thick, dark red sauce, sweet and tangy at the same time. Wait until the end of the grilling time to apply this sauce, because the sugar in it scorches easily.

2 tablespoons unsalted butter

1 yellow onion, cut into ⅛-inch (3-mm) dice (page 30)

2 cloves garlic, minced (page 34)

1 cup (8 fl oz/250 ml) tomato ketchup

1 cup (8 fl oz/250 ml) American-style tomato-based chili sauce

½ cup (3½ oz/105 g) firmly packed light brown sugar

½ cup (4 fl oz/125 ml) cider vinegar

2 tablespoons spicy brown mustard

2 tablespoons Worcestershire sauce

½ teaspoon red hot-pepper sauce

MAKES ABOUT 3 CUPS (24 FL OZ/750 ML)

CHEF'S TIP
When grilling, barbecue sauce should be applied to food only during the last 10 minutes of cooking—5 minutes on each side—to prevent the sugar in the sauce from burning and developing undesirable charred bits on the surface of the grilled food.

1 Sauté the vegetables
Place a heavy-bottomed nonreactive saucepan over medium heat and add the butter. When the butter has melted and the foam begins to subside, add the onion and cook, stirring often, until the onion is golden, about 6 minutes. Stir in the garlic and cook until the garlic is fragrant, about 1 minute.

2 Simmer the sauce
Add the ketchup, chili sauce, brown sugar, vinegar, mustard, and Worcestershire sauce. Bring to a simmer, stirring often. Reduce the heat to medium-low to keep the sauce at a slow simmer. Cook uncovered, stirring often with a wooden spatula to scrape up any sauce that would otherwise stick to the bottom and sides of the pan and start to scorch, until the sauce is thick and reduced by about one-fourth, about 30 minutes. Remove from the heat and season with the hot-pepper sauce. (When using hot-pepper sauce, it is best to add it at the end of cooking, as its flavor dissipates with long simmering.)

3 Adjust the seasonings
Taste the sauce; it should have a nice balance of tangy, salty, sweet, and spicy, with no flavors dominating. As the flavorings are so bold, you probably won't need to adjust the seasonings. However, a little more hot-pepper sauce could lend a spicier edge to the sauce.

4 Use or store the sauce
Use the sauce right away, or store it. Let the sauce cool to room temperature. Transfer it to a covered container and refrigerate for up to 2 weeks. The large quantities of acids and sugar in the sauce discourage bacterial growth, so barbecue sauce keeps well. (During outdoor-grilling season, make a double batch of sauce to store in the refrigerator.) The sauce does not freeze well.

RECOMMENDED USES
Serve with your favorite grilled or barbecued meats and poultry, with grilled salmon, or barbecued oysters. (The sauce is too highly seasoned for most other seafood.)

Barbecue Sauce Variations

This collection of barbecue sauces illustrates how easily Kansas City–Style Barbecue Sauce (page 68) lends itself to variation once you've learned the basic method of simmering ingredients together to intensify their flavors. Spicy brown mustard stars in the South Carolina sauce, and is combined with molasses to give the Memphis type a slightly bitter note. Georgia's sauce gets fruity sweetness from peach preserves. Chiles add heat to the Texas and chipotle sauces. And although barbecue is a traditionally American style of cooking, there's no need to confine yourself to the American pantry. Savory hoisin and aromatic ginger combine in an Asian version that rivals the others.

South Carolina–Style Mustard Sauce

The addition of hard apple or pear cider mellows the bite of the mustard. Serve this tangy sauce with smoked pork shoulder or poultry.

In a heavy, nonreactive saucepan over medium heat, melt 2 tablespoons unsalted butter. Add 1 finely diced yellow onion and sauté until golden, about 6 minutes. Add 2 minced garlic cloves and sauté until fragrant, about 1 minute. Add ⅓ cup (2½ oz/75g) firmly packed brown sugar, ¼ cup (2 fl oz/60 ml) cider vinegar, 1 cup (8 oz/250 g) spicy brown mustard, and ½ cup (4 fl oz/125 ml) hard apple cider, hard pear cider, or nonalcoholic apple cider. Bring to a simmer, then reduce the heat to medium-low and simmer for 5 minutes. Stir in ½ teaspoon red hot-pepper sauce.

Adjust the seasonings and use or store the sauce.

MAKES ABOUT 2 CUPS (16 FL OZ/500 ML)

Memphis-Style Barbecue Sauce

Memphis barbecue restaurants offer spareribs either dry (seasoned with spice rub only) or wet (served with lots of spicy sauce). Here is a first-rate example of a sauce to use for the latter.

In a heavy, nonreactive saucepan over medium heat, melt 2 tablespoons unsalted butter. Add 1 finely diced yellow onion and sauté until golden, about 6 minutes. Add 2 minced garlic cloves and sauté until fragrant, about 1 minute. Add 1 cup (8 fl oz/250 ml) tomato ketchup, 1 cup (8 fl oz/250 ml) American-style chili sauce, ½ cup (5½ oz/170 g) light molasses, ½ cup (4 fl oz/125 ml) cider vinegar, ¼ cup (2 oz/60 g) spicy brown mustard, 2 tablespoons Worcestershire sauce, and ½ teaspoon freshly ground pepper. Bring to a simmer, then reduce the heat to medium-low and simmer for 30 minutes. Stir in ½ teaspoon red hot-pepper sauce.

Adjust the seasonings and use or store the sauce.

MAKES ABOUT 3 CUPS (24 FL OZ/750 ML)

Georgia-Style Barbecue Sauce

This sauce, which is excellent brushed on spareribs, pork chops, or chicken, gets a mild kick from the addition of bourbon.

In a heavy, nonreactive saucepan over medium heat, melt 2 tablespoons unsalted butter. Add 1 finely diced yellow onion and sauté until golden, about 6 minutes. Add 2 minced garlic cloves and sauté until fragrant, about 1 minute. Add 1 cup (8 fl oz/250 ml) tomato ketchup, 1 cup (8 fl oz/250 ml) American-style chili sauce, ½ cup (5 oz/155 g) peach preserves, ⅓ cup (3 fl oz/80 ml) cider vinegar, ⅓ cup (3 fl oz/80 ml) bourbon, and 3 tablespoons spicy brown mustard. Bring to a simmer, then reduce the heat to medium-low and simmer for 30 minutes. Stir in ½ teaspoon red hot-pepper sauce.

Adjust the seasonings and use or store the sauce.

MAKES ABOUT 3 CUPS (24 FL OZ/750ML)

Texas-Style Barbecue Sauce

Chili powder (a blend of chiles, cumin, oregano, and other spices) gives this sauce authentic Texas flavor.

In a heavy-bottomed, nonreactive saucepan over medium heat, melt 2 tablespoons unsalted butter. Add 3 oz (90 g) sliced bacon, cut into 1-inch (2.5-cm) pieces, and sauté until the bacon is crisp and browned, about 6 minutes. Using a slotted spoon, transfer the bacon to paper towels to cool and drain, leaving the fat in the saucepan. Finely chop the cooked bacon.

Add 1 finely diced yellow onion and ½ diced green bell pepper (capsicum) to the pan and sauté until the onion is golden, about 6 minutes. Add 2 minced garlic cloves and 1 seeded and finely chopped jalapeño chile and sauté until the garlic is fragrant, about 1 minute. Add 2 tablespoons chili powder and stir for 15 seconds to release the aroma and flavor of the powder.

Return the bacon to the pan along with 2 cups (16 fl oz/500 ml) canned tomato purée, ½ cup (3½ oz/105 g) firmly packed light brown sugar, ½ cup (4 fl oz/125 ml) cider vinegar, 2 tablespoons spicy brown mustard, and 2 tablespoons Worcestershire sauce. Bring to a simmer, then reduce the heat to medium-low and simmer for 30 minutes. Stir in ½ teaspoon green hot-pepper sauce.

Adjust the seasonings and use or store the sauce. Because it contains meat, the sauce will keep for only 5 days.

MAKES ABOUT 3 CUPS (24 FL OZ/750 ML)

Ginger Barbecue Sauce

Try this familiar, yet exotic-flavored sauce on grilled pork.

Peel 1 large piece of fresh ginger. Use the small shredding holes on a box grater-shredder to shred ½ cup (2 oz/60 g) fresh ginger into a bowl, catching any juice. Next, heat 2 tablespoons canola oil in a heavy-bottomed saucepan over medium heat. Add 6 chopped green (spring) onions (white and tender green parts) and sauté until the onions are golden, about 6 minutes. Add 2 minced garlic cloves and the shredded ginger and juice and sauté for 30 seconds.

Add 1 cup (8 fl oz/250 ml) tomato ketchup, ½ cup (4 fl oz/125 ml) water, ⅔ cup (5 fl oz/160 ml) hoisin sauce, ¼ cup (2 fl oz/60 ml) unseasoned rice vinegar, and 2 tablespoons soy sauce to the pan. Bring to a simmer, then reduce the heat to medium-low and simmer for 5 minutes. Stir in ½ teaspoon red hot-pepper sauce.

Adjust the seasonings and use or store the sauce.

MAKES ABOUT 2⅔ CUPS (21 FL OZ/660 ML)

Chipotle Barbecue Sauce

Chipotle chiles, smoke-dried jalapeños here packed in a vinegar-tomato sauce called *adobo*, bring a whiff of wood smoke and plenty of heat to this sauce.

Wearing latex gloves, finely chop 2 canned chipotle chiles in adobo sauce. Next, melt 2 tablespoons unsalted butter in a heavy-bottomed, nonreactive saucepan over medium heat. Add 3 oz (90 g) sliced bacon, cut into 1-inch (2.5 cm) pieces, and sauté until the bacon is crisp and browned, about 6 minutes. Using a slotted spoon, transfer the bacon to paper towels to cool and drain, leaving the fat in the saucepan. Finely chop the cooked bacon.

Add 1 finely diced yellow onion and ½ diced green bell pepper (capsicum) to the pan and sauté until the onion is golden, about 6 minutes. Add 2 minced garlic cloves and sauté until the garlic is fragrant, about 1 minute.

Return the bacon to the pan along with 2 cups (16 fl oz/500 ml) canned tomato purée, ½ cup (3½ oz/105 g) firmly packed light brown sugar, ½ cup (4 fl oz/125 ml) cider vinegar, 2 tablespoons spicy brown mustard, and 2 tablespoons Worcestershire sauce.

Bring to a simmer, then reduce the heat to medium-low and simmer for 30 minutes. Stir in ½ teaspoon green hot-pepper sauce.

Adjust the seasonings and use or store the sauce. Because it contains meat, the sauce will keep for only 5 days.

MAKES ABOUT 3 CUPS (24 FL OZ/750 ML)

Demi-glace

This version of a French mother sauce is much simpler than the classic. The latter requires making a roux-based sauce and a stock and simmering both for hours. Simply reduce meat stock to its intensely flavored essence. When it gels, cut it into cubes to have on hand for enriching sauces or making a quick stock.

1 **Reduce the stock**
In a large saucepan over high heat, bring the stock to a boil. Boil uncovered, skimming off any foam or scum that forms on the surface, until it is dark brown, has thickened to a syrupy consistency, and has a rich, meaty flavor, about 1 hour. Be careful when reducing stock for such a long period. If you don't pay attention, it can cross the line from being perfectly thickened to being perfectly burned. Set a timer or stay in the kitchen to help avoid this. Take special care in the final minutes of cooking, too, checking on the thickness of the reduction frequently. You should have ½ cup (4 fl oz/125 ml).

2 **Use or cool the concentrated stock**
Use a heatproof silicone spatula to scrape every last drop of precious demi-glace out of the saucepan into a small bowl. Use the sauce right away, or let it cool and store for later. Refrigerate until the sauce is firm, then use a small knife to ease the gelatinous mixture out of the bowl; it will resemble brown Jell-O. Cut into ¼-inch (6-mm) cubes. If you need a measured liquid amount for a recipe, melt it first in a microwave or small saucepan for accuracy.

3 **Store the concentrated stock**
Because so much water is cooked out of the stock, and water is needed for bacterial growth, this sauce keeps well and can be refrigerated for up to 2 weeks. Unless you are planning to use the entire batch right away, however, it is best to freeze the concentrated stock to use as needed. Wrap each cube in a small piece of plastic wrap. Put the cubes in a small locking plastic bag, squeeze out any excess air, and freeze for up to 3 months.

2 qt (2 l) Brown Meat Stock (page 20)

MAKES ABOUT ½ CUP (4 FL OZ/125 ML)

CHEF'S TIP
A small amount of concentrated stock will be left clinging to the saucepan at the end of reducing the stock. Add about 2 cups (16 fl oz/500 ml) water, cover, and bring to a boil over high heat. The steam trapped by the lid will loosen the stock on the pan sides. Scrape the stock into the water, whisk well to dissolve, and use as brown meat stock.

RECOMMENDED USES
As a sauce for steaks and chops, as a flavor enhancer for meat-based stews and sauces such as Red Wine Sauce (page 74), or dissolved in hot water to make a quick stock.

Red Wine Sauce

Here is a new take on classic Bordelaise sauce, which traditionally calls for a bottle of expensive Bordeaux wine and plenty of time. Today's cooks need a quicker, lighter, but equally flavorful version, which is what is presented here. Change the stock you use depending on what you are serving: meat stock for red meat, or poultry stock for poultry or pork.

3 tablespoons cold unsalted butter

1 small shallot, diced (page 31)

4 cups (32 fl oz/1 l) Brown Meat Stock (page 20) or Brown Poultry Stock (page 18)

1½ cups (12 fl oz/375 ml) hearty red wine such as a Zinfandel or Syrah

1 tablespoon reduced-sodium soy sauce

1½ teaspoons tomato paste

¼ teaspoon dried thyme, crumbled

½ bay leaf

1 tablespoon Demi-glace (page 73 or purchased), optional

2 tablespoons cold water

1 tablespoon cornstarch (cornflour)

¼ teaspoon salt

⅛ teaspoon freshly ground pepper

MAKES ABOUT 2 CUPS (16 FL OZ/500 ML)

CHEF'S TIP
When cooking with wine, use only wine that's good enough to drink by itself. Better yet, pour the same wine at the table when you serve the dish.

RECOMMENDED USES
As a light-bodied sauce for grilled or panfried beef, especially sliced flank, skirt, or hanger steak; tri-tip roast; roast beef; or roasted poultry.

1 Cook the shallot
In a heavy-bottomed saucepan over medium heat, melt 1 tablespoon of the butter (keep the remaining 2 tablespoons butter refrigerated). When the butter has melted and the foam begins to subside, add the shallot and cook, stirring occasionally, until browned, about 3 minutes.

2 Reduce the liquids
Add the stock, wine, soy sauce, tomato paste, thyme, and bay leaf. (The tomato paste is used as a coloring agent, and not as a flavoring, so don't add too much.) If you have it, add the Demi-glace for an extra boost of meaty flavor. Increase the heat to high and bring to a boil. Cook, uncovered, until the sauce is reduced to 2 cups, about 30 minutes. The timing will depend on the heat of the stove and size of the pan. Tilt the pan occasionally to estimate the amount of liquid remaining.

3 Thicken the sauce
Reduce the heat to very low, so that the sauce just simmers (very small bubbles). If you are new to using a slurry, turn to page 38. Pour the water into a small bowl. Sprinkle the cornstarch over the water and stir to dissolve, making a slurry. Whisk a little of the slurry into the simmering sauce and bring to a boil. Cook just until the sauce thickens, about 1 minute. If the sauce is not sufficiently thickened, add a little more slurry and let boil again. If the sauce seems too thick, thin it with additional stock or water. Remove and discard the bay leaf. If you prefer not to have flecks of shallot in the finished sauce, strain the sauce through a fine-mesh sieve.

4 Mount the sauce with butter
To find out more about mounting a sauce with butter, turn to page 41. Cut the 2 tablespoons cold butter into small cubes and place the sauce over very low heat. A few cubes at a time, whisk the butter into the sauce. It will become shiny and slightly thickened.

5 Adjust the seasonings and serve
Stir in the salt and pepper and taste the sauce; it should taste rich, meaty, and of the wine you used. If it's a little dull, stir in a little more salt or pepper until the flavors are nicely balanced. Serve right away.

Brown Butter–Caper Sauce

Butter that is cooked until lightly browned (but not burned) has a marvelous nutty taste that is perfectly balanced by tangy capers. Despite its simplicity, this sauce is packed with the flavors of both ingredients, and a generous spoonful drizzled over the top of the food you're serving is all that's needed.

1 Prepare the capers
Drain the capers in a sieve, rinse under running cold water, and then drain again. This removes some of the excess salt from the brine. (If using larger capers, coarsely chop them.)

2 Brown the butter
Place a frying pan over medium-high heat and add the butter. The butter will froth; as the foam subsides, watch it carefully. The butter will turn light brown, about 2 minutes. At this point, immediately take the pan off the heat. The French call this *beurre noisette*, literally "hazelnut butter," for its nut-brown color and nutty flavor. If the butter is cooked too long it will burn and become bitter.

3 Add the capers
Return the pan to the heat and carefully add the capers to the butter—they could cause spattering—and cook until they are heated through, about 30 seconds. Do not overcook. Stir in the salt and pepper and remove the pan from the heat.

4 Adjust the seasonings
Taste the sauce; it should taste nutty from the browned butter and piquant from the capers. If the sauce tastes a bit dull, stir in a little salt and pepper until you are happy with the flavor balance.

5 Serve the sauce
Spoon an equal amount of the melted butter and capers over each serving of food. This sauce has a lovely transparency, but when served with pale foods, the plate can look washed out. To add color, sprinkle each serving with parsley. For extra flavor, serve with lemon wedges. Serve right away.

2 tablespoons capers, preferably small nonpareil capers

4 tablespoons (2 oz/60 g) unsalted butter

⅛ teaspoon salt

Pinch of freshly ground pepper

Minced fresh flat-leaf (Italian) parsley and lemon wedges, optional

MAKES ABOUT ⅓ CUP (3 FL OZ/80 ML)

CHEF'S TIP
If you are just learning to make brown butter, keep a wide bowl of cold water near the stove. If the butter appears to be getting too brown, immerse the base of the pan in the water to halt the cooking. Be sure to wipe off the moisture before returning the pan to the stove.

RECOMMENDED USES
This sauce is perfect with panfried fish fillets, but you can also try it with panfried pork tenderloin medallions or chicken breasts.

Emulsions & Butter Sauces

When a fat (such as butter or oil) and a liquid (such as eggs or vinegar) are vigorously mixed, the fat is broken up into tiny bubbles that are suspended throughout the liquid and a thick emulsion is formed. Unemulsified butter can also form a delicious sauce on its own, combined with a few flavorful ingredients. You'll find examples of both types of sauces on the pages that follow.

Hollandaise Sauce

Delicate hollandaise should taste primarily of butter, with only a hint of lemon. This makes a strong argument for using the best butter available, like a European-style one with a high butterfat content and distinctive flavor. Note that this recipe includes uncooked eggs. For more details, see page 11.

1 Clarify the butter

To find out more about clarifying butter, turn to page 36. Cut the butter into small pieces and put them in a small saucepan on the stove top. Turn the heat to medium and bring the butter to a boil, watching it carefully so that it doesn't boil over. Reduce the heat to medium-low and cook the butter for 1 minute, but no longer, to evaporate the excess water in the butter. Remove the pan from the heat and let the butter stand for 2 minutes. Using a large metal spoon, skim the foam from the surface of the butter and discard it; these are impurities that have risen to the top. Carefully pour the clear yellow liquid into a heatproof measuring cup, leaving behind the creamy white milk solids in the bottom of the saucepan. You should have ⅔ cup (5 fl oz/160 ml) clarified butter.

2 Separate the eggs

If you are unsure how to separate eggs, turn to page 37. Take the eggs from the refrigerator (they are easiest to separate when cold). Have 3 small bowls ready. Working over the first bowl, crack 1 egg and pass the yolk back and forth between the shell halves, allowing the white to drop into the bowl. Drop the yolk into the second bowl. Transfer the white to the third bowl. Repeat with the remaining 3 eggs. Save the egg whites for another use. Cover the yolks with plastic wrap to prevent a skin from forming.

3 Set up a double boiler

Pour 1 inch (2.5 cm) water into a saucepan and heat over medium heat until small bubbles form on the surface of the water. (This is a simmer.) Create a double boiler by placing a metal bowl in the top of the saucepan. Make sure that the bowl fits snugly in the rim and that its bottom does not touch the simmering water. Reduce the heat to maintain a bare simmer and put the yolks in the bowl. ›

1 cup (8 oz/250 g) unsalted European-style butter

4 cold large eggs

2 tablespoons water

2–3 teaspoons fresh lemon juice

¼ teaspoon salt

⅛ teaspoon freshly ground pepper, preferably white pepper

MAKES ABOUT 1 CUP (8 FL OZ/250 ML)

CHEF'S TIP
To rid the clarified butter of all milk solids, pour the separated butter with the milk solids into a heatproof measuring cup and refrigerate for about 4 hours. Then, invert the butter into a saucepan and, using paper towels, wipe away any traces of the milk solids from the firm butterfat. Melt the clarified butter before using.

RECOMMENDED USES
Turn to page 85 for creative ideas for using hollandaise in recipes.

4>

4 Combine the egg yolks with water

Add the 2 tablespoons water to the egg yolks and, using a handheld mixer on high speed or a whisk, beat until the yolks are slightly thickened and a pale yellow, about 30 seconds. This helps aerate the yolks and begin emulsification.

5 Begin to add the butter slowly

Using pot holders, carefully lift the bowl slightly and peer into the pan to make sure the water is barely simmering; you want to warm the sauce, not cook it, and if the heat under the saucepan is too high, the egg yolks can curdle. With the mixer on low speed or a hand whisk, mix constantly while gradually drizzling the clarified butter, about 1 teaspoon at a time, into the yolks. Take your time adding the butter—especially at the beginning—or the sauce could separate. Once half of the butter has been added, you can mix in the remainder at a slightly faster pace. But don't rush; your patience will be rewarded with a smooth sauce.

6 Check the consistency of the sauce

The finished sauce will be smooth, glossy, and barely warm; do not overcook it. If the sauce appears to be separated into semisolid and liquid parts, you have added the butter too quickly. If you detect this problem before adding more than one-fourth of the butter, whisk 1 tablespoon cold water into the sauce; this may bring it back together. For a more serious case, you may still be able to save it.

7 Fix a broken sauce, if necessary

To find out more about how to fix a broken hollandaise, turn to page 42. Pour the separated sauce into the measuring cup holding the remaining melted butter. Wash and dry the bowl. Whisk 2 fresh egg yolks and 1 tablespoon water in the bowl until thickened, about 30 seconds, and place over gently simmering water in the saucepan. Now, at a much slower pace than you previously added the butter, whisk the broken sauce and melted butter mixture into the yolks in the bowl. (For even better results re-emulsifying the sauce, use a blender. See the recipe for Blender Hollandaise on page 87.) ›

CHEF'S TIP

As you become more proficient at making hollandaise, you can try making it in a saucepan alone, rather than over simmering water. If you do, be careful to keep the heat extremely low. A heat diffuser—a piece of equipment that sits directly on the burner to dissipate the heat—is especially helpful.

8 Strain the sauce

Strain the sauce through a fine-mesh sieve set over a larger bowl. This removes any bits of cooked egg white or chalazae, thin white cords attached to the yolk, that may have been clinging to the yolk. Egg whites cook at a lower temperature than yolks, so warm egg-based sauces should always be strained to remove the whites and ensure a smooth sauce.

CHEF'S TIP

If the sauce curdles and flecks of semisolid, darker yellow yolk are visible, the heat was too high. You can process the sauce in a blender to dissolve the bits of yolk, but the sauce will still have a cooked egg flavor. It may be better to discard the curdled sauce and start over.

9 Adjust the seasonings

Whisk in 2 teaspoons of the lemon juice and the salt and pepper, and then taste the sauce. If it tastes a little flat, add more salt, pepper, or lemon juice (keeping in mind that hollandaise is not a lemon sauce) a little at a time until the flavor is to your liking.

10 Serve or hold the sauce

Serve the sauce right away, or hold it. Hollandaise is never served hot, and the food served with it should be warm enough to heat the sauce on contact. To hold the sauce for up to 30 minutes, cover the bowl with plastic wrap. Place the bowl in a frying pan of barely simmering water over the lowest possible heat. The egg yolks will curdle if they reach temperatures higher than 180°F (82°C), so make sure that the water in the pan does not simmer rapidly or boil. Whisk well before serving. To keep hollandaise for longer, transfer it to a widemouthed thermos and cap it. Use the sauce within 2 hours.

Serving Ideas

Hollandaise is a surprisingly complex sauce. In flavor, it is luscious but subtle; in texture, it is rich but delicate. This complexity allows it to marry with a range of foods. Hollandaise pairs well with the understated flavors of poached or steamed foods that allow its buttery flavor to shine. It can also accompany rich foods, acting as an echo to their richness, or it can cloak plainly cooked vegetables for a nice counterpoint.

Hollandaise with eggs (top left)
Serve hollandaise with poached eggs on toasted English muffins—with or without Canadian bacon—to make the hearty brunch classic eggs Benedict.

Hollandaise with fish (left)
Serve hollandaise or its tarragon-scented cousin, Béarnaise Sauce (page 87), with poached salmon or other fish as an elegant main course suitable for company.

Hollandise with vegetables (above)
Serve hollandaise with steamed or boiled asparagus, broccoli, or cauliflower to dress up a simple vegetable side dish.

Hollandaise Sauce Variations

Once you've mastered classic Hollandaise Sauce on page 81, you will be able to make other sauces that call for the same thick, stable emulsion of butter and eggs. For example, you can fold whipped cream into hollandaise for a lighter consistency but richer flavor, or you can add red bell pepper purée to hollandaise for a sauce that calls for less butter and is thus more healthful. Adding a reduction of wine, tarragon, and shallots to hollandaise produces another traditional sauce, béarnaise, while the addition of tomato to béarnaise results in the equally traditional pastel Choron sauce. Finally, you can also use your blender to whip up the signature emulsion that defines a hollandaise.

Whipped Cream Hollandaise Sauce
Sauce Mousseline

Serve this light and airy sauce with steamed vegetables or poached fish.

Before beginning, using a balloon whisk or a handheld mixer on high speed, whip ¼ cup (2 fl oz/60 ml) heavy (double) cream in a chilled small bowl until stiff, pointed peaks form when the whisk is lifted.

Follow the recipe to make the hollandaise. In step 9, after adding the lemon juice, salt, and pepper, use a heatproof spatula to pile the whipped cream on top of the sauce and then fold it in: Cut down through both mixtures, sweep the spatula along the bottom of the bowl, and bring the spatula up and over the top, carrying some of the sauce with it. Give the bowl a quarter turn, and repeat until the streaks disappear and the two mixtures are just blended. Too much stirring will deflate the cream and make the sauce less fluffy.

Adjust the seasonings and serve or hold the sauce.

MAKES ABOUT 1¼ CUPS (10 FL OZ/310 ML)

Orange Hollandaise Sauce
Sauce Maltaise

Magenta-fleshed blood oranges are traditional in this sauce, whose French name refers to the celebrated oranges of Malta. If you can't find them, use a Valencia or other juice orange.

Before beginning, grate the zest from only half of 1 blood orange. Cut the orange in half on its equator and juice both halves; pour through a fine-mesh sieve into a 1-cup (8–fl oz/250-ml) heatproof glass measuring cup to total ¼ cup (2 fl oz/60 ml). Heat on high in a microwave oven until the juice is reduced to 2 tablespoons, about 3 minutes. Alternatively, boil in a small, heavy-bottomed saucepan until reduced; watch carefully, as this small amount of juice can quickly caramelize.

Follow the recipe to make the hollandaise. In step 9, whisk in the reduced orange juice and the orange zest in place of the lemon juice.

Adjust the seasonings and serve or hold the sauce.

MAKES ABOUT 1 CUP (8 FL OZ/250 ML)

Red Bell Pepper Hollandaise Sauce

This lovely dark rose sauce pairs well with fish or shellfish.

Before beginning, roast 1 red bell pepper (capsicum); (see page 121). Remove and discard the skin, ribs, and seeds, then purée the roasted red bell pepper in a blender or food processor. You should have ⅓ cup (3 fl oz/80 ml) purée. In a saucepan over low heat or in a microwave oven on medium, heat the purée just until warm.

Follow the recipe to make the hollandaise, but reduce the amount of clarified butter to ⅓ cup (3 fl oz/80 ml). In step 5, after slowly whisking in the clarified butter, whisk in the warm bell pepper purée 1 tablespoon at a time.

Continue with the recipe. In step 9, substitute ⅛ teaspoon red hot-pepper sauce for the white pepper.

Adjust the seasonings and serve or hold the sauce.

MAKES ABOUT 1⅓ CUPS (11 FL OZ/340 ML)

Béarnaise Sauce

Prepare this versatile sauce for serving with grilled meats and fish, vegetables, and poached eggs.

Before beginning, in a small nonreactive saucepan over high heat, combine ¼ cup (1½ oz/45 g) finely diced shallots, 3 tablespoons dry white wine such as Sauvignon Blanc, 3 tablespoons white wine vinegar, 2 tablespoons chopped fresh tarragon, and ¼ teaspoon freshly ground coarse black pepper. Bring to a boil. Cook until the liquid has almost completely evaporated and the mixture is syrupy, about 2 minutes. This can be done up to 1 hour ahead; hold the mixture at room temperature.

Follow the recipe to make the hollandaise. In step 9, instead of seasoning with lemon juice and white pepper, whisk in the shallot mixture. Adjust the seasonings and serve or hold the sauce.

MAKES ABOUT 1 CUP (8 FL OZ/250 ML)

Tomato Béarnaise Sauce
Sauce Choron

Adding tomato paste to béarnaise sauce gives it a lovely pastel orange-pink color and savory flavor that complements grilled veal or pork chops or meaty fish such as snapper or sea bass.

Before beginning, in a small nonreactive saucepan over high heat, combine ¼ cup (1½ oz/45 g) finely diced shallots, 3 tablespoons dry white wine such as Sauvignon Blanc, 3 tablespoons white wine vinegar, 2 tablespoons chopped fresh tarragon, and ¼ teaspoon freshly ground coarse black pepper. Bring to a boil. Cook until the liquid has almost completely evaporated and the mixture is syrupy, about 2 minutes. This can be done up to 1 hour ahead; hold the mixture at room temperature.

Follow the recipe to make the hollandaise. In step 9, instead of seasoning with lemon juice and white pepper, whisk in the shallot mixture and 1 tablespoon high-quality tomato paste. Adjust the seasonings and serve or hold the sauce.

MAKES ABOUT 1 CUP (8 FL OZ/250 ML)

Blender Hollandaise Sauce

A blender's blade aerates the sauce less than beaters, making it firmer in texture than hollandaise made with a hand mixer. Even with the blender, remember to add the butter slowly in the beginning.

Instead of setting up a double boiler in step 3, place the yolks and water in a blender and pulse to combine. With the machine running, slowly add the clarified butter in a steady stream through the hole in the lid. As the sauce thickens, occasionally stop the machine and scrape down the sides of the container.

Continue with the recipe to strain the sauce (or you can skip this step, as any cooked whites will have been pulverized by the blades). Adjust the seasonings and serve or hold the sauce.

MAKES ABOUT 1½ CUPS (12 FL OZ/375 ML)

Mayonnaise

Homemade mayonnaise, a mixture of fresh eggs and flavorful olive oil, is much richer and creamier than its commercial counterpart. Here are three different ways to prepare it: by blender, mixer, and food processor. Note that this recipe includes uncooked eggs. For more details, see page 11.

Blender Method

1 Prepare the ingredients

For this method you'll need only 1 egg. Place the uncracked egg in a bowl, then fill the bowl with very warm tap water. Let stand for 3–5 minutes to warm the egg. Cold ingredients do not emulsify as readily as room-temperature ones. Crack the egg in a dry bowl, check for shell bits, and then pour it into a blender. Add the lemon juice and mustard. Mix the canola and olive oils together in a 2-cup (16–fl oz/500-ml) glass measuring cup.

2 Slowly blend the ingredients

With the blender running, very slowly add the mixed oils in a steady stream through the opening in the lid. As the blender runs, the mixture will emulsify, gradually thickening, increasing in volume, and changing from bright yellow to opaque cream. Occasionally stop the machine and scrape down the sides of the container. The blending process should take at least 1½ minutes. After the first half of the oil has been added, you can add the second half slightly faster.

3 Adjust the seasonings

Transfer the mayonnaise to a serving dish or a storage container. Stir in the salt and pepper and then taste the mayonnaise. For a creamier mayonnaise, whisk in the water. If you prefer a tangier mayonnaise, add more mustard or lemon juice. Salt or pepper can enliven a dull mayonnaise. Add any seasonings sparingly until the flavor is to your liking.

4 Serve or store the mayonnaise

Use the mayonnaise right away, or store it. Cover and refrigerate for up to 5 days. This recipe makes a substantial amount of fresh mayonnaise—considering that it keeps for only 5 days—but it is difficult to make a smaller quantity. See the ideas on page 93 for ways to use the mayonnaise. ›

---

1 or 2 large eggs

1 tablespoon fresh lemon juice

1 teaspoon Dijon mustard

¾ cup (6 fl oz/180 ml) canola or soybean oil, at room temperature

¾ cup (6 fl oz/180 ml) olive oil, at room temperature

¼ teaspoon salt, preferably fine sea salt

⅛ teaspoon freshly ground pepper, preferably white pepper

1 tablespoon water, optional

MAKES 1¾ CUPS (14 FL OZ/430 ML)

CHEF'S TIP

Instead of separating 2 eggs for their yolks (and possibly wasting the whites), you can use 1 whole egg when making mayonnaise in a blender or food processor. The machines' blades cut through the egg so rapidly that it is quickly absorbed without need for the emulsifying power of the extra yolk.

RECOMMENDED USES
In cold salads, such as potato salad or coleslaw, or savory dips, or as a condiment for steamed or boiled artichokes or other green vegetables.

A combination of light-flavored vegetable oil and olive oil (not extra-virgin) makes the most stable and best-tasting mayonnaise.

Placing bowls on top of
a folded damp kitchen
towel helps keep them
steady on the surface as
you work.

Electric Mixer Method

1 Separate the eggs

If you are not sure how to separate eggs, turn to page 37. Take 2 eggs from the refrigerator (they are easiest to separate when cold). Have 3 small bowls ready. Working over the first bowl, crack 1 egg and pass the yolk back and forth between the shell halves, allowing the white to drop into the bowl. Drop the yolk into the second bowl. Transfer the white to the third bowl before cracking the next egg. Save the egg whites for another use.

2 Prepare the ingredients

Transfer the egg yolks to a medium glass bowl, then place the bowl in a larger bowl of warm tap water. Stir the egg yolks with a rubber spatula just until they lose their chill; use your finger to test the temperature. Cold ingredients do not emulsify as readily as room-temperature ones. Stir the lemon juice and mustard into the yolks. To help steady the bowl, place it on a folded damp kitchen towel. Mix the canola and olive oils together in a 2-cup (16–fl oz/500-ml) glass measuring cup.

3 Slowly beat the ingredients

Using a handheld mixer on high speed, start beating the egg yolk mixture. While beating constantly, add the oils in a very slow, steady drizzle. As you beat, the sauce will emulsify, gradually thickening, increasing in volume, and changing from bright yellow to opaque cream. The beating process should take at least 1½ minutes. After the first half of the oil has been added, you can add the second half slightly faster. (If the sauce "breaks" into semisolid and liquid parts and looks curdled, you have added the oils too quickly. Turn to page 43 for instructions on fixing a broken mayonnaise).

4 Adjust the seasonings

Transfer the mayonnaise to a serving dish or a storage container. Stir in the salt and pepper and then taste the mayonnaise. For a creamier mayonnaise, whisk in the water. If you prefer a tangier mayonnaise, add more mustard or lemon juice. Salt or pepper can enliven a dull mayonnaise. Add any seasonings sparingly until the flavor is to your liking.

5 Serve or store the mayonnaise

Use the mayonnaise right away, or store it. Cover and refrigerate for up to 5 days. This recipe makes a substantial amount of fresh mayonnaise—considering that it keeps for only 5 days—but it is difficult to make a smaller quantity. See the ideas on page 93 for ways to use the mayonnaise.

Food Processor Method

1 Prepare the ingredients
For this method you'll need only 1 egg. Place the uncracked egg in a bowl, then fill the bowl with very warm tap water. Let stand for 3–5 minutes to warm the egg. Cold ingredients do not emulsify as readily as room-temperature ones. Crack the egg into a bowl, check for shell bits, and then pour it into a food processor. Add the lemon juice and mustard. Mix the canola and olive oils together in a 2-cup (16–fl oz/500-ml) glass measuring cup.

2 Slowly process the ingredients
With the processor running, very slowly add the mixed oils in a steady stream through the feed tube. As the processor runs, the mixture will emulsify, gradually thickening, increasing in volume, and changing from bright yellow to opaque cream. As the mayonnaise thickens, occasionally stop the machine and scrape down the sides of the container. The processing should take at least 1½ minutes. After the first half of the oil has been added, you can add the second half of the oil slightly faster.

3 Adjust the seasonings
Transfer the mayonnaise to a serving dish or a storage container. Stir in the salt and pepper and then taste the mayonnaise. For a creamier mayonnaise, whisk in the water. If you prefer a tangier mayonnaise, add more mustard or lemon juice. Salt or pepper can enliven a dull mayonnaise. Add any seasonings sparingly until the flavor is to your liking.

4 Serve or store the mayonnaise
Use the mayonnaise right away, or store it. Cover and refrigerate for up to 5 days. This recipe makes a substantial amount of fresh mayonnaise—considering that it keeps for only 5 days—but it is difficult to make a smaller quantity. See the ideas on page 93 for ways to use the mayonnaise.

CHEF'S TIP
Be sure all ingredients are at room temperature when making mayonnaise; cold ingredients make the sauce more likely to break.

Serving Ideas

Mayonnaise serves so many uses, it's easy to forget that it's a sauce. It adds rich, savory flavor and an appealing smoothness to foods that are normally a little bland or dry on their own. It is also an essential ingredient in any number of dips, sandwiches, and salads. Mayonnaise's thick, luscious consistency also makes it ideal for both scooping with artichoke leaves and spreading on a bun with a juicy burger.

Mayonnaise with fries (top left)
Use mayonnaise to accompany slender *pommes frites*, or French fries, in the European fashion. Aioli (page 94), or garlic mayonnaise, is another good choice for accompanying fried foods like calamari.

Mayonnaise in sandwiches (left)
Serve plain mayonnaise or any of the variations on pages 94–95 as a condiment for sandwiches—here, grilled chicken with arugula and tomato on a crunchy baguette.

Garnishing mayonnaise (above)
When serving mayonnaise plain as a dip, dress up the presentation with a sprinkle of paprika or cayenne pepper.

Mayonnaise Variations

Mayonnaise (page 88) is based on creating a stable emulsion of eggs and oil, which you now know how to make with a blender, an electric mixer, and a food processor. All three methods can also be used to whip up the half dozen variations presented here. When the weather is warm and your herb garden is flourishing, you can stir in parsley, chives, and dill for a mildly flavored alternative to plain mayonnaise. In contrast, the addition of the more robustly flavored garlic, pesto, or wasabi delivers a bolder sauce. Capers and sour pickles add a piquancy to two classic mayonnaise-based sauces for seafood, tartar and rémoulade.

Lemon-Herb Mayonnaise

Just about any combination of herbs you like can be stirred into mayonnaise. Serve this sauce with chilled seafood such as poached salmon or as a dip for fresh vegetables.

Follow the recipe to make the mayonnaise. After beating in the oils, stir in the grated zest of 1 lemon, 1 tablespoon minced fresh flat-leaf (Italian) parsley, 1 tablespoon minced fresh chives, and, if desired, 1 tablespoon minced fresh dill.

Continue with the recipe to adjust the seasonings and serve or store the mayonnaise.

MAKES ABOUT 1¾ CUPS (14 FL OZ/430 ML)

Aioli *Garlic Mayonnaise*

This is a modern take on the pounded Provençal sauce, which is traditionally served with an array of cooked vegetables for dipping.

Follow the recipe to make the mayonnaise, replacing the pure olive oil with ¾ cup (6 fl oz/180 ml) extra-virgin olive oil. After beating in the oils, stir in 2 or 3 minced garlic cloves.

Continue with the recipe to adjust the seasonings and serve or store the mayonnaise.

MAKES ABOUT 1¾ CUPS (14 FL OZ/430 ML)

CHEF'S TIP
Do not try to make mayonnaise, or any of the variations, with a stand mixer; the bowl is too large for the volume of sauce.

Pesto Mayonnaise

Spread this mayonnaise on sandwiches made with Italian cured meats or grilled summer vegetables.

Follow the recipe to make the mayonnaise. After beating in the oils, stir 2 tablespoons Basil Pesto (page 109) or one of the pesto variations (page 114–15) into the mayonnaise.

Continue with the recipe to adjust the seasonings, keeping in mind that the pesto itself is salty, and serve or store the mayonnaise.

MAKES ABOUT 1¾ CUPS (14 FL OZ/430 ML)

Tartar Sauce

This is a classic sauce for sautéed, grilled, or deep-fried fish.

Follow the recipe to make the mayonnaise. After beating in the oils, mix 3 tablespoons chopped gherkin pickles, 3 tablespoons rinsed and drained capers (preferably nonpareil, or chopped large ones), and 1 tablespoon chopped fresh flat-leaf (Italian) parsley into the mayonnaise.

Continue with the recipe to adjust the seasonings, substituting ⅛ teaspoon red hot-pepper sauce for the white pepper, and serve or store the sauce.

MAKES ABOUT 2 CUPS (16 FL OZ/500 ML)

CHEF'S TIP
If you are unsure about the freshness of your eggs, put them in a bowl of cold water. If the eggs sink to the bottom and lie on their sides, they are fresh. If they float or stand on one end, they are past their prime.

Rémoulade

In New Orleans, rémoulade often has a vinaigrette base, but the classic French sauce is made from mayonnaise. Serve with fish and shellfish.

Follow the recipe to make the mayonnaise, using 1 teaspoon Creole or spicy brown mustard in place of the Dijon mustard. After beating in the oils, mix in 1 tablespoon chopped gherkin pickle, 1 tablespoon rinsed and drained capers (preferably nonpareil, or chopped large ones), 1 tablespoon minced fresh tarragon, 1 tablespoon minced fresh chives, 1 teaspoon anchovy paste, and 1 minced garlic clove.

Continue with the recipe to adjust the seasonings, substituting ⅛ teaspoon red hot-pepper sauce for the white pepper, and serve or store the sauce.

MAKES ABOUT 2 CUPS (16 FL OZ/500 ML)

Wasabi-Lime Mayonnaise

Powdered wasabi gives this variation a spicy flavor. It is a zesty partner for raw oysters or a grilled tuna sandwich.

Before beginning, in a small bowl, mix 2 tablespoons wasabi powder with 2 tablespoons water to make a smooth paste. Let stand for 5 minutes.

Follow the recipe to make the mayonnaise, substituting 1 tablespoon fresh lime juice for the lemon juice and omitting the mustard. After beating in the oils, whisk the wasabi paste into the mayonnaise 1 teaspoon at a time, tasting as you go, until the spice level suits your taste. Mix in the grated zest of 1 lime.

Continue with the recipe to adjust the seasonings and serve or store the mayonnaise.

MAKES ABOUT 1¾ CUPS (14 FL OZ/430 ML)

Beurre Blanc
White Wine Butter Sauce

Rich with butter, beurre blanc is similar to hollandaise. But unlike hollandaise, it starts with a heady blend of dry white wine, vinegar, and shallot. These acidic ingredients contribute to the sauce in two ways: they help hold the emulsion together, and they give the pale yellow sauce a distinctive flavor.

1 Dice the shallot
If you are not sure how to dice a shallot, turn to page 31. Cut the shallot in half lengthwise and pull off the peel. Place a shallot half flat side down on a cutting board and make a series of parallel lengthwise cuts about ¼ inch (6 mm) apart, stopping at the root. Holding the knife parallel to the board, make another series of cuts just to the root end, perpendicular to the first, also ¼ inch apart. Now cut the shallot crosswise into small dice. Repeat with the second half if needed to measure out 2 tablespoons diced shallot.

2 Prepare the herb, if using
This pale sauce can benefit from a colorful garnish. Tarragon, with a subtle anise flavor, or dill, with its distinct aromatic flavor, is a good match for the sauce. Remove the leaves from the stems and discard the stems. Gather the leaves into a small pile. Using a sharp chef's knife, mince the leaves. You should have about 1 teaspoon minced herb. Transfer the minced herb to a small bowl, cover with a damp paper towel, and set aside.

3 Cook the wine with the shallot
In a small nonreactive saucepan over high heat, combine the wine, vinegar, and diced shallot. (Wine and vinegar are acidic ingredients that can react with an aluminum or uncoated cast-iron pan, giving an off flavor to the final sauce.) Bring the mixture to a boil and cook until the liquid has reduced to 2 tablespoons, about 5 minutes. This liquid, or any liquid evaporated and reduced by boiling, is called a *reduction*. Tilt the pan occasionally to estimate the amount of liquid remaining. Remove the saucepan from the heat and let cool for about 30 seconds. If the sauce is too hot, the butter will simply melt and not mount the mixture to a creamy consistency. ›

1 shallot

2 sprigs fresh tarragon or dill, optional

1 cup (8 fl oz/250 ml) dry white wine, such as Sauvignon Blanc or Pinot Grigio

2 tablespoons white wine vinegar

1 cup (8 oz/250 g) cold unsalted butter

¼ teaspoon salt

⅛ teaspoon freshly ground pepper, preferably white pepper

MAKES ABOUT ⅔ CUP (5 FL OZ/160 ML)

CHEF'S TIP
Leftover beurre blanc can be chilled for up to 1 day and then used like a compound butter (page 104). Put small pieces of the cold sauce on top of hot food. It will melt and form a sauce.

RECOMMENDED USES
Serve with grilled or sautéed seafood, as a dip for artichokes, or as a sauce for steamed asparagus, broccoli, or even Brussels sprouts.

4 Cut the butter into cubes

While the wine mixture is cooling, cut the cold butter into ½-inch (12-mm) cubes. Cut each stick of butter in half lengthwise into slices ½ inch thick. Turn the slices 90 degrees and cut again ½ inch thick. Finally, cut the butter crosswise into ½-inch cubes.

5 Mount the sauce with butter

To find out more about mounting a sauce with butter, turn to page 41. Turn on the heat to very low. You merely want to warm the mixture, not cook it. Place the saucepan over the heat. Add a few cold butter cubes to the shallot-wine reduction and whisk until the cubes are almost completely incorporated. Continue adding the butter a few cubes at a time and whisking until the mixture transforms into an ivory-colored sauce with the consistency of thick heavy (double) cream.

6 Adjust the seasonings

Stir in the salt and pepper and then taste the sauce. It should taste both tangy and creamy, with a nice acidity from the wine. If you feel it tastes a little dull, stir in a bit more salt and pepper until the flavors are nicely balanced. Keep in mind that if you plan to use the herbs, they will add additional flavor.

7 Strain and garnish the sauce

Like hollandaise, beurre blanc is served warm but never steaming hot. To help it maintain its temperature, strain it into a warmed bowl. Just before straining the sauce, fill the serving bowl with hot tap water and let stand to warm the bowl. Pour out the water and dry the bowl, then immediately strain the sauce through a fine-mesh sieve into the warmed bowl, being sure not to press the shallots through the sieve.

8 Serve or hold the sauce

If using, sprinkle the chopped herbs over the sauce. Serve the beurre blanc right away, or hold it. To hold the sauce for up to 2 hours, place the bowl in a warm place in the kitchen, perhaps near the stove. If the sauce starts to thicken, it can be thinned with a tablespoon or two of hot white wine or water.

Beurre Blanc Variations

By mastering Beurre Blanc (page 97), you have learned three invaluable techniques for making similar sauces: how to reduce ingredients over high heat to concentrate their flavors, how to mount a sauce with butter to increase its volume and give it an appealing sheen, and how to strain a sauce to yield a smooth finish. You can now make a more intensely flavored beurre blanc based on red wine, or you can substitute balsamic vinegar for the white wine vinegar for a sweeter sauce. And come winter, when oranges and lemons are filling the markets, think about flavoring this versatile butter sauce with citrus zest.

Beurre Rouge
Red Wine Butter Sauce

The flavor of the wine will be intensified as it reduces, so use a red wine without heavy oak aging. Serve the sauce with veal chops or beef steaks.

Follow the recipe to make the beurre blanc, but in step 3, replace the white wine and white wine vinegar with 1 cup hearty red wine (such as a Zinfandel, Syrah, or Shiraz–Cabernet Sauvignon blend) and 2 tablespoons red wine vinegar.

Continue with the recipe to mount the sauce with butter, adjust the seasonings, strain, and serve or hold the sauce.

MAKES ABOUT ⅔ CUP (5 FL OZ/160 ML)

Citrus Beurre Blanc

This light and refreshing version of beurre blanc complements steamed or boiled green vegetables and all types of fish and shellfish.

Follow the recipe to make the beurre blanc; you won't need the optional herbs. Then, after straining the sauce in step 7, stir in the grated zest of 1 orange, lemon, or lime.

Continue with the recipe to serve or hold the sauce.

MAKES ABOUT ⅔ CUP (5 FL OZ/160 ML)

Balsamic Beurre Blanc

Since the flavor of a balsamic vinegar is altered by cooking, don't use a pricey long-aged one here. The sweet tang of balsamic pairs well with lamb.

Follow the recipe to make the sauce, but in step 2, mince the leaves from 1 sprig rosemary (½ teaspoon minced) instead of the tarragon (optional). Then, in step 3, replace the white wine vinegar with 2 tablespoons balsamic vinegar.

Continue with the recipe to mount the sauce with butter, adjust the seasonings, strain, and serve or hold the sauce, garnishing with the rosemary, if desired.

MAKES ABOUT ⅔ CUP (5 FL OZ/160 ML)

Vinaigrette

Oil and vinegar with salt and pepper—that's all there is to a traditional vinaigrette sauce. These two liquids don't willingly blend, but when properly handled, they emulsify to form an unctuous, tangy, vibrant sauce that will lightly dress the components of a salad or other preparation with a thin, glistening, flavorful coating.

1 Whisk the vinegar and salt

In a medium rounded bowl, combine the vinegar and salt. To steady the bowl, place it on a folded damp kitchen towel. The salt is added before the oil because it dissolves more easily in vinegar alone. Using an elongated whisk, and using a circular motion, whisk the vinegar and salt until the salt begins to dissolve. Whisk in the mustard, if using. (In addition to adding flavor to a vinaigrette, mustard acts as an emulsifier, an ingredient that helps to stabilize and hold together the blend of oil and vinegar. Using mustard gives a vinaigrette more thickness and body.)

2 Whisk in the oil

Gradually add the oil while whisking rapidly in a circular motion. As you whisk, the ingredients will emulsify, gradually thickening, increasing in volume, and changing in appearance from transparent to opaque.

3 Adjust the seasonings

Whisk in the pepper. Although salt was added in the first step, you should taste the final vinaigrette and season with additional salt and pepper, if needed. Do not taste the vinaigrette by itself; it will probably taste too sour. For a more accurate evaluation of flavor, dip a piece of the lettuce or other food the vinaigrette will dress into it, shake off the excess, and taste the vinaigrette and food together. If you like your vinaigrette more tangy, add more vinegar or mustard. If you prefer a more subtle flavor, whisk in a bit more oil.

4 Serve or store the vinaigrette

Use the vinaigrette right away, or store it. To store the vinaigrette for up to 5 days, transfer it to a covered container and refrigerate it. The olive oil will thicken when chilled. About 30 minutes before using, remove the vinaigrette from the refrigerator or place the container in a bowl of warm water just until the oil "melts" and comes to room temperature. Any emulsification will separate upon standing, but vinaigrette can usually be simply whisked or shaken to thicken and re-emulsify it.

3 tablespoons red wine vinegar, preferably aged wine vinegar

¼ teaspoon salt

½ teaspoon Dijon mustard, optional

¾ cup (6 fl oz/180 ml) extra-virgin olive oil

⅛ teaspoon freshly ground pepper

MAKES ABOUT 1 CUP (8 FL OZ/250 ML)

CHEF'S TIP
Although a whisk is the classic tool for emulsifying ingredients, it is not the only option when making a vinaigrette. You can also use a fork or a handheld mixer or even vigorously shake the ingredients in a tightly covered jar or bottle. For the thickest vinaigrette, use a blender as described on page 102.

RECOMMENDED USES
To dress all types of salads, from simple tossed greens to boiled green beans to poached leeks; as a sauce for poached or grilled seafood.

Vinaigrette Variations

The following vinaigrettes are all based on a combination of an acid and oil, but they are quite different from one another. One is fruity, another gets tang from blue cheese, and a third has a distinctly Asian flavor. Once you've learned to make a great classic Vinaigrette (page 101), you can start to experiment with flavors. The traditional proportion of oil to vinegar is four parts oil to one part vinegar, but this ratio can change depending on the vinegar's level of sharpness. For example, balsamic is mild, so less oil is needed for balance. Pure (not extra-virgin) olive oil and light-bodied vegetable oils such as canola or soybean can be used when a distinct olive taste is not desirable.

Blender Vinaigrette

The blender's blades break up the oil into more tiny droplets than a whisk does, and the increased number of droplets gives this vinaigrette a smoother and thicker mouthfeel.

Put the vinegar, salt, and mustard (if using) in a blender. Process to combine. With the blender running, gradually add the oil in a steady stream through the hole in the lid. Season with the pepper.

Continue with the recipe to adjust the seasonings and serve or store the vinaigrette.

MAKES ABOUT 1 CUP (8 FL OZ/250 ML)

Roquefort, Sherry & Walnut Vinaigrette

Use this vinaigrette to dress green salads with roasted beets, or any time you want a thick but light-bodied blue cheese dressing.

Follow the recipe to make the vinaigrette, but in step 1, replace the red wine vinegar with 3 tablespoons sherry vinegar and omit the optional mustard. In step 2, replace the olive oil with ¾ cup (6 fl oz/ 180 ml) walnut oil. After whisking in the oil, stir in 3 oz (90 g) Roquefort or other blue-veined cheese, crumbled, and ½ minced shallot.

Continue with the recipe to adjust the seasonings, keeping in mind that the Roquefort cheese itself is salty, and serve or store the vinaigrette.

MAKES ABOUT 1¼ CUPS (10 FL OZ/310 ML)

Raspberry-Walnut Vinaigrette

Sprinkle a salad dressed with this vinaigrette with toasted chopped walnuts to underscore the flavor of the walnut oil. For the fullest flavor, use French walnut oil or a domestic brand that is labeled "toasted."

Follow the recipe to make the vinaigrette, but in step 1, replace the red wine vinegar with 3 tablespoons raspberry vinegar and omit the optional mustard. In step 2, replace the olive oil with ¾ cup (6 fl oz/180 ml) walnut oil.

Continue with the recipe to adjust the seasonings and serve or store the vinaigrette.

MAKES ABOUT 1 CUP (8 FL OZ/250 ML)

Lemon-Shallot Vinaigrette

This bright yellow vinaigrette is a tasty dressing for a seafood salad.

Before beginning, zest and juice 1 lemon. Set the zest aside and measure out 3 tablespoons lemon juice.

Follow the recipe to make the vinaigrette, but in step 1, replace the red wine vinegar with the lemon juice and then whisk in the zest. Proceed with step 2 to whisk in the oil, then stir in 1 tablespoon minced shallot.

Continue with the recipe to adjust the seasonings and serve or store the vinaigrette.

MAKES ABOUT 1 CUP (8 FL OZ/250 ML)

Asian Vinaigrette

Ginger juice is now available in some markets. Instructions for making it from fresh ginger are included here. Use this dressing for mildly bitter greens or napa cabbage slaw.

Before beginning, peel 1 large piece fresh ginger. Use the large shredding holes on a box grater-shredder to shred ¼ cup (1 oz/30 g) ginger into a small bowl. Squeeze the ginger in your hand over the bowl to extract the juice. You should have about 1 tablespoon ginger juice. Discard the shredded ginger.

Follow the recipe to make the vinaigrette, but in step 1, replace the red wine vinegar with 3 tablespoons unseasoned rice vinegar, and add the ginger juice and 1 tablespoon soy sauce; omit the optional mustard. In step 2, replace the olive oil with ⅔ cup (5 fl oz/ 160 ml) canola or soybean oil combined with 1 tablespoon Asian sesame oil.

Continue with the recipe to adjust the seasonings, keeping in mind that the soy sauce is salty, and serve or store the vinaigrette.

MAKES ABOUT 1 CUP (8 FL OZ/250 ML)

Orange-Tarragon Vinaigrette

The bulk of this reduced-fat, slightly sweet vinaigrette comes from an orange-juice reduction, which requires less oil to balance it than vinegar does. This pairs well with chicken or shrimp (prawns), or steamed asparagus or artichokes.

Before beginning, bring 1 cup (8 fl oz/ 250 ml) fresh orange juice to a boil in a small saucepan over high heat. Cook until the orange juice is reduced to ½ cup (4 fl oz/125 ml), about 10 minutes. Let cool completely.

Follow the recipe to make the vinaigrette, but in step 1, replace the red wine vinegar with 3 tablespoons balsamic vinegar, whisking it with the reduced orange juice, mustard, and salt. In step 2, whisk in only ¼ cup (2 fl oz/60 ml) olive oil. Stir in 2 teaspoons finely chopped fresh tarragon.

Continue with the recipe to adjust the seasonings and serve or store the vinaigrette.

MAKES ABOUT 1 CUP (8 FL OZ/250 ML)

½ cup (4 oz/125 g) unsalted butter, at room temperature

For parsley-lemon compound butter *(beurre maître d'hôtel)*

2 tablespoons minced fresh flat-leaf (Italian) parsley

Grated zest of 1 lemon

1 tablespoon fresh lemon juice

For blue cheese compound butter

3 oz (90g) Roquefort or other blue-veined cheese, at room temperature

For olive compound butter

¼ cup (1½ oz/45 g) finely chopped black Mediterranean olives such as Kalamata

⅛–¼ teaspoon salt

Pinch of freshly ground pepper

MAKES ABOUT ½ CUP (4 OZ/125 G)

CHEF'S TIP

If you're short on time and want to use butter that is still cold from the refrigerator, thinly slice it and use an electric mixer to beat the butter for a couple of minutes to soften it. Then, add the flavorings and beat to combine.

RECOMMENDED USES
On meats, especially steak; tossed with steamed or boiled vegetables, such as new potatoes or green beans.

Compound Butter

The term *compound* refers to the putting together of parts. Here, the parts are softened butter and three different flavoring options from which to choose. The flavored butter is shaped into a log, for slicing into pats, and refrigerated to firm the butter and marry the flavors. The flavors in the butter will bloom when the butter melts over hot food.

1 **Mix the butter and flavorings**
In a medium bowl, combine the butter with the flavorings of your choice to make parsley-lemon butter, blue cheese butter, or olive butter. Mash and fold the mixture until it is smooth and uniformly mixed. A rubber spatula does the best job of blending the softened butter and the flavorings into a uniform consistency, but a wooden spatula or spoon can also be used.

2 **Adjust the seasonings**
Taste the butter. Add salt or pepper to enliven dull-tasting mixtures, keeping in mind that some of the ingredients—blue cheese, olives—are already salty and will permeate the mixture as it sits.

3 **Shape the flavored butter**
Place a 12-inch (30-cm) square of waxed paper or plastic wrap on your work surface. Scrape the butter out of the bowl onto the waxed paper, about 2 inches (5 cm) from the edge nearest you, shaping the butter into a horizontal strip about 8 inches (20 cm) long and 2 inches (5 cm) wide. Fold the edge of the paper nearest you over to cover the butter, then roll up the waxed paper to shape the butter into a cylinder. Pick up the cylinder by the 2 ends of waxed paper. Twist the ends of the paper in opposite directions—like wrapping a piece of saltwater taffy—and the paper will tighten to shape the butter into a compact log. Refrigerate the butter until it is firm and the flavors have married, at least 2 hours.

4 **Serve or store the flavored butter**
When ready to serve, unwrap the butter and cut off a slice ¼ inch (6 mm) thick (about 1 tablespoon) for each serving; any more may be too rich. Place the pats of butter on top of hot food and they will melt and coat the food. The wrapped butter can be refrigerated for up to 1 week. To store for up to 2 months, freeze it. The frozen compound butter can be used without thawing, since it will melt fairly quickly when it touches hot food. To ease cutting frozen butter into pats, run a sharp knife under hot water to heat it, dry it quickly, and then slice the butter.

5

Salsas, Purées & Relishes

The sauces in this chapter represent a more modern array of sauces than the heavily French-influenced sauces in the previous chapters. These recipes, which are based on fresh herbs, vegetables, and fruits, rely on the bold flavor of the ingredients and little added fat for their appeal. They are generally quick to prepare and brightly colored, and they represent a palette of flavors from all around the world.

Basil Pesto

There are few kitchen tasks more aromatic than grinding basil and garlic with nuts, cheese, and olive oil into verdant green pesto. In Italian, *pesto* means "pounded." The original recipe uses a mortar and pestle, but many cooks turn to a food processor or blender for convenience. All three methods are given here.

Food processor method

1 Prepare the ingredients

Finely grate the cheese using a fine rasp grater or the small grating holes of a box grater-shredder. Toasting the nuts is an optional step, but it will deepen their flavor. In a small, dry frying pan over medium heat, spread the pine nuts in a single layer. Cook, stirring often, until the nuts are fragrant and just starting to color, 3–5 minutes. (You don't want to leave the nuts unattended while toasting as they easily burn.) Transfer the nuts to a plate to stop the cooking and let cool. With the motor of a food processor running, drop the garlic cloves through the feed tube. Turn off the machine, add the cheese and pine nuts, and pulse briefly.

2 Process the ingredients

Add the basil and then turn on the machine. Pour the oil in a thin, steady stream through the feed tube and process to make a moderately thick paste. Stop the machine occasionally and use a rubber spatula to scrape the ingredients from the sides of the work bowl down into the bowl to help them blend evenly.

3 Adjust the seasonings

Stir in the salt and pepper and taste the pesto; it should taste primarily of fresh basil, with accents of garlic, nuts, and cheese. If it tastes flat, add more cheese, salt, or pepper until the flavors are nicely balanced.

4 Use or store the pesto

Use the pesto right away, or store it. Transfer the pesto to a container with a cover. Pour a thin layer of olive oil over the entire surface to slow the discoloration, cover, and refrigerate for up to 1 week. Before using, bring to room temperature and stir well. >

2 oz (60 g) *pecorino romano* or Parmigiano-Reggiano cheese, or 1 oz (30 g) of each cheese

¼ cup (1 oz/30 g) pine nuts

2 cloves garlic

2 cups (2 oz/60 g) packed fresh basil leaves, preferably sweet basil or Genoese basil, well dried in a salad spinner

½ cup (4 fl oz/125 ml) extra-virgin olive oil

¼ teaspoon salt

⅛ teaspoon freshly ground pepper

MAKES ABOUT 1 CUP (8 FL OZ/250 ML)

CHEF'S TIP

To keep basil pesto a vibrant green, many chefs add a couple tablespoons of flat-leaf (Italian) parsley leaves to their formula. Parsley doesn't darken the way basil does when it is pounded or cut.

Mortar & pestle method

1 **Prepare the ingredients**
Finely grate the cheese using a fine rasp grater or the small grating holes of a box grater-shredder. Toasting the nuts is an optional step, but it will deepen their flavor. In a small, dry frying pan over medium heat, spread the pine nuts in a single layer. Cook, stirring often, until the nuts are fragrant and just starting to color, 3–5 minutes. Transfer the nuts to a plate to stop the cooking and let cool.

2 **Pound the garlic, basil, and pine nuts**
Put the garlic cloves in a mortar and mash them several times with the pestle. A small handful at a time, add the basil leaves to the mortar and use firm pressure to pound and mash them with the pestle to break up the leaves into a shapeless mass. This could take several minutes, so don't be discouraged. As you pound, use your other hand to hold the mortar in place. Gradually add the pine nuts, using the pestle to crush and mash them into the pesto.

3 **Stir in the cheese and oil**
Transfer the basil mixture to a bowl, scraping the mortar clean with a rubber spatula. Stir in the cheese. Still stirring, pour in the oil in a thin, steady stream to make a moderately thick paste.

4 **Adjust the seasonings**
Stir in the salt and pepper, then taste the pesto; it should taste primarily of fresh basil, with accents of garlic, nuts, and cheese. If it tastes flat, add more cheese, salt, or pepper until the flavors are nicely balanced.

5 **Use or store the pesto**
Use the pesto right away, or store it. Transfer the pesto to a container with a cover. Pour a thin layer of olive oil over the entire surface to slow the discoloration, cover, and refrigerate for up to 1 week. Before using, bring to room temperature and stir well. ›

CHEF'S TIP
Some cooks find that bruising and mashing the garlic and basil with a mortar and pestle brings out their flavors better than the sharp blades of a blender or food processor.

Blender method

1 Prepare the ingredients
Finely grate the cheese using a fine rasp grater or the small grating holes of a box grater-shredder. Toasting the nuts is an optional step, but it will deepen their flavor. In a small, dry frying pan over medium heat, spread the pine nuts in a single layer. Cook, stirring often, until the nuts are fragrant and just starting to color, 3–5 minutes. (You don't want to leave the nuts unattended while toasting, as they easily burn.) Transfer the nuts to a plate to stop the cooking and let cool.

CHEF'S TIP

Basil tends to become stronger in flavor and more bitter as it matures. For the best-tasting pesto, look for bunches with small, young leaves.

2 Blend the ingredients
With the blender motor running, drop the garlic cloves through the hole in the lid. Then, add the oil and then the nuts. With the machine still running, add a handful of basil and blend until it is puréed. In batches, add the remaining basil, occasionally stopping the machine and using a rubber spatula to push the basil leaves into the purée. If the pesto becomes too thick to process, add additional oil to loosen the mixture. The pesto should have a moderately thick consistency. Stop the blender from time to time and scrape down the sides of the container with the spatula.

3 Adjust the seasonings
Transfer the mixture to a bowl and use the spatula to stir in the cheese. Stir in the salt and pepper and taste the pesto; it should taste primarily of fresh basil, with accents of garlic, nuts, and cheese. If it tastes flat, add more cheese, salt, or pepper until the flavors are nicely balanced.

4 Use or store the pesto
Use the pesto right away, or store it. Transfer the pesto to a container with a cover. Pour a thin layer of olive oil over the entire surface to slow the discoloration, cover, and refrigerate for up to 1 week. Before using, bring to room temperature and stir well.

Recommended uses

Pesto is a perennially popular sauce with a seemingly limitless number of uses. It's best known as a pasta sauce, but its chunky yet unctuous texture and fresh, aromatic flavor give it a high degree of versatility. Pesto works nicely as a relish for all sorts of grilled foods, ranging from fish to steak, or it can dress up a plain, typically dry food like bread (think crostini) or potato (think gnocchi or baked potato).

Pesto as a spread (top left)
Use pesto as a topping for baguette slices that have been brushed with olive oil and toasted or grilled.

Pesto as a relish (left)
A grilled meaty fish like tuna or a strong-flavored one like salmon stands up well to the vibrant flavors of pesto. Other natural partners are grilled lamb, beef, and chicken.

Pesto as a pasta sauce (above)
When used as a pasta sauce, pesto should be thinned slightly with a little of the pasta cooking water so that it will cling better to the pasta. Thin strand pasta like spaghetti or angel hair and smooth, plump potato gnocchi are classic matches.

Pesto Variations

Now that you have mastered classic Basil Pesto (page 109) made by mortar and pestle, blender, or food processor, you can try making other types of pesto. Italy's northwest region of Liguria is home to the classic version, but different regions have their own recipes, including ones that call for arugula or mint in place of the basil. Here, I also offer a New World take: cilantro pesto, with flavors borrowed from Mexican cuisine. Various grating cheeses (semihard *pecorino*, or Gruyère for a Provençal version), different nuts, and varying amounts of garlic can be used, too. One constant, however, is flavorful extra-virgin olive oil.

Pesto with Walnuts & Pecorino

Pecorino and walnuts make a slightly sharper-tasting sauce than pesto made with Parmigiano-Reggiano and pine nuts.

Follow the food processor method, mortar and pestle method, or blender method for making the pesto, replacing the pine nuts with ¼ cup (1 oz/30 g) finely chopped walnuts and using all *pecorino romano* cheese in place of any Parmigiano-Reggiano cheese.

Adjust the seasonings, then serve or store the pesto.

MAKES ABOUT 1 CUP (8 FL OZ/250 ML)

Mint Pesto

Spread this aromatic pesto on lamb for the last 10 minutes of roasting or grilling, or use as a zesty condiment.

Follow the food processor method, mortar and pestle method, or blender method for making the pesto, replacing the basil with 2 cups (2 oz/60 g) packed fresh mint leaves.

Adjust the seasonings, then serve or store the pesto.

MAKES ABOUT 1 CUP (8 FL OZ/250 ML)

CHEF'S TIP
Fresh herbs are easiest to mince, chop, or crush when they are completely dry. After rinsing well, I like to whirl them in a salad spinner to remove every trace of rinsing water.

Rosemary-Walnut Pesto

Colorful and fragrant, this pesto is an excellent accompaniment to grilled chops and steaks.

Follow the food processor method, mortar and pestle method, or blender method for making the pesto, replacing the pine nuts with ¼ cup (1 oz/30 g) chopped walnuts and replacing the basil with 1¾ cups (1¾ oz/50 g) packed fresh flat-leaf (Italian) parsley leaves and ¼ cup (⅓ oz/10 g) chopped fresh rosemary.

Adjust the seasonings, then serve or store the pesto.

MAKES ABOUT 1 CUP (8 FL OZ/250 ML)

Arugula Pesto

Toss pasta with this naturally peppery pesto and grilled shrimp (prawns).

Rinse well and spin dry 2 cups (2 oz/60 g) packed arugula (rocket) leaves. Remove any tough stems from the arugula leaves and discard the stems.

Follow the food processor method, mortar and pestle method, or blender method for making the pesto, replacing the basil with the cleaned arugula leaves.

Adjust the seasonings, then serve or store the pesto.

MAKES ABOUT 1 CUP (8 FL OZ/250 ML)

Cilantro Pesto

Use this pesto to accompany roasted pork loin or grilled chicken.

Follow the food processor method, mortar and pestle method, or blender method for making the pesto, replacing the pine nuts with ¼ cup (1 oz/30 g) shelled pumpkin seeds. Add 1 seeded and chopped jalapeño chile along with the garlic and replace the basil with 2 cups (2 oz/60 g) packed fresh cilantro (fresh coriander) leaves. For the cheese, use ½ cup (2 oz/60g) grated *cotija* or all *pecorino romano* or *pecorino sardo* in place of any Parmigiano-Reggiano cheese.

For an extra boost of flavor, stir in the grated zest of 1 lime and 1 tablespoon fresh lime juice.

Adjust the seasonings, then serve or store the pesto.

MAKES ABOUT 1 CUP (8 FL OZ/250 ML)

CHEF'S TIP
Pesto can also be frozen for up to 3 months. If you're planning to freeze it, don't add the cheese. Wait until the pesto thaws, then stir in the cheese and adjust the seasonings just before using.

Pistou

This is the Provençal version of pesto. While its traditional use is as a soup flavoring (add a dollop to each serving), it also complements grilled fish.

Follow the food processor method, mortar and pestle method, or blender method for making the pesto, replacing the pine nuts with ¼ cup (1 oz/30 g) sliced (flaked) natural or blanched almonds, and replacing the *pecorino romano* and Parmigiano-Reggiano with ½ cup (2 oz/60 g) finely shredded Gruyère cheese.

Adjust the seasonings, then serve or store the pesto.

MAKES ABOUT 1 CUP (8 FL OZ/250 ML)

Tomato Salsa

All good cooking relies on quality ingredients, but this is especially true when making this seasonal salsa, since it consists entirely of raw ingredients. When done right, with juicy tomatoes at the height of their summer harvest, a bright taste of lime, and sweet, aromatic white onion, it delivers a fresh, satisfying flavor.

1 Seed and dice the tomatoes
If you are not sure how to seed a tomato, turn to page 35. Using a chef's or serrated knife, cut each tomato in half crosswise through its "equator." Squeeze each half gently and use a finger to help scoop out the seed sacs. Discard the seed sacs. One at a time, place the seeded tomato halves cut side down on the work surface and cut into slices ¼ inch (6 mm) thick. Cut the slices into ¼-inch (6-mm) strips. Finally, cut the strips crosswise into ¼-inch dice.

2 Prepare the chile
If you are new to working with chiles, turn to page 40. Wear a latex glove, if desired, on the hand that touches the chile, and take care not to touch your face while working. With a small sharp knife, cut the jalapeño lengthwise into quarters. With the tip of the knife, cut the stem, ribs, and seeds from the jalapeño. Reserve the seeds and ribs. They contain most of the *capsaicin*, which carries spiciness, and they can be used to adjust the seasoning. (The ribs are spicier than the seeds.) Cut the quarters into strips, then cut the strips crosswise into dice. Gather the diced jalapeño on the cutting board. Using a chef's knife, rock the knife rhythmically over the chile flesh to cut it into fine, even pieces, or *mince*.

3 Mix the salsa
In a bowl, mix together the tomatoes, jalapeño, onion, cilantro (if using; in my house at least, the cilantro is optional), lime juice, and garlic, taking care not to crush the tomatoes. Season with the salt. Let stand at room temperature for 15 minutes to blend the flavors.

4 Adjust the seasonings
Taste the salsa. If it seems too mild, add some of the reserved jalapeño seeds. If they don't do the trick, mince the reserved jalapeño ribs and add them, too. If the salsa tastes bland, stir in a bit more lime juice or salt until the flavors seem nicely balanced to your taste.

5 Serve or hold the salsa
Serve the salsa right away, or hold it. The salsa tastes best the day it is made, as the flavors become muddled if it is held longer. Cover the salsa with plastic wrap and refrigerate for up to 12 hours. Serve chilled or at room temperature.

3 tomatoes, about 1 lb (500 g) total weight

1 jalapeño chile

½ white onion, finely diced (page 30)

2 teaspoons minced fresh cilantro (fresh coriander), optional

Juice of ½ lime

1 clove garlic, minced (page 34)

½ teaspoon salt

MAKES ABOUT 2 CUPS (16 FL OZ/500 ML)

CHEF'S TIP
I like to use white onions in raw preparations such as fresh salsas and other uncooked relishes. They are less sharply flavored than yellow onions. If the onion still tastes too sharp to you, soak the diced pieces in ice water for 15 minutes, then drain and pat dry thoroughly before using.

RECOMMENDED USES
As a condiment for Mexican dishes or grilled foods such as flank steak or halibut, or served with tortilla chips as a dip.

Salsa Variations

After making Tomato Salsa (page 116), you'll gain confidence in your knife skills and ability to season a mixture to your personal taste. Then, you can begin to expand your repertory with the following six salsas. A cooked tomato salsa allows you to use canned tomatoes during the cold months when good fresh ones can't be found. A mix of black beans and corn results in a rustic, robust salsa for an early autumn table, while tomatillos give an acidic tang and a very different color palette. When full fruit flavors are what you want, pineapple and mango make well-rounded tropical salsas, and in the dead of winter, an orange salsa spiked with spicy chiles can brighten a menu.

Cooked Tomato Salsa

Canned tomatoes can be used in salsas as long as the other ingredients are also cooked. Spoon the salsa over Mexican dishes or use as a dip for tortilla chips.

Drain 1 can (28 oz/875 g) diced tomatoes in juice. Place a frying pan over medium heat. Add 1 tablespoon olive oil and heat until the surface just shimmers. Add ½ finely diced white onion and sauté until translucent, about 4 minutes. Add 1 minced jalapeño and 1 minced garlic clove and cook until the garlic is fragrant, about 1 minute. Add the drained tomatoes and cook, stirring occasionally, just until heated through. Transfer to a bowl and let cool.

Add to the cooled tomato mixture the juice of ½ lime, 2 teaspoons minced fresh cilantro (fresh coriander), and a pinch of salt and mix gently but thoroughly. Let stand for 15 minutes, adjust the seasonings, and serve or hold the salsa.

MAKES 2 CUPS (16 FL OZ/500 ML)

Pineapple-Mint Salsa

This salsa is well suited to grilled pork.

In a bowl, mix together 2 cups (12 oz/ 375 g) diced fresh pineapple, 1 minced jalapeño chile, 2 tablespoons minced shallot, 1½ tablespoons minced fresh mint, 2 tablespoons fresh lime juice, ½ teaspoon salt, and ¼ teaspoon freshly ground pepper.

Let stand for 15 minutes, adjust the seasonings, and serve or hold the salsa.

MAKES ABOUT 2 CUPS (16 FL OZ/500 ML)

Black Bean & Corn Salsa

In addition to being a great dip for tortilla chips, this salsa pairs well with grilled tuna.

In a bowl, mix together 1 seeded and diced tomato, 1 minced jalapeño, ½ finely diced white onion, 1 minced garlic clove, 1 can (15 oz/470 g) rinsed and drained black beans or 1¼ cups (9 oz/280 g) cooked black beans, and ¾ cup (4½ oz/140 g) fresh (from about 1½ ears) or thawed frozen corn kernels.

Let stand for 15 minutes, adjust the seasonings, and serve or hold the salsa.

MAKES ABOUT 3 CUPS (24 FL OZ/750 ML)

Tomatillo Salsa

Choose tomatillos of a similar size so they cook at the same rate. This salsa especially complements chicken.

Remove and discard the paper husks from 1 lb (500 g) tomatillos. Bring a saucepan of lightly salted water to a boil over high heat. Add the tomatillos and reduce the heat so the water is at a steady simmer. Cook, uncovered, until the tomatillos are barely tender and are an even olive green, about 12 minutes, depending on their size. Do not overcook, because if the tomatillos burst, it will affect the texture of the final salsa. If smaller tomatillos are tender before the larger ones, use a slotted spoon to transfer them to a bowl.

In a food processor, combine the tomatillos, 1 minced jalapeño chile, ½ diced white onion, 2 tablespoons minced fresh cilantro (fresh coriander), 2 tablespoons fresh lime juice, and ½ teaspoon salt. Pulse about 10 times until the salsa is relatively smooth, but still has some texture.

Let stand for 15 minutes, adjust the seasonings, and serve or hold the salsa.

MAKES ABOUT 2 CUPS (16 FL OZ/500 ML)

Mango Salsa

The sweet, spicy, and pungent flavors of this fruit salsa marry well with grilled salmon.

Pit, peel, and dice 3 ripe mangoes: Stand each mango on a narrow side, with the stem end facing you. Using a sharp knife, cut down the length of the fruit, about 1 inch (2.5 cm) from the stem and just grazing the large, flat pit. Repeat on the other side of the pit. Peel the 2 large pieces of mango and cut into ¾-inch (2-cm) dice.

In a bowl, mix together the diced mango, 1 minced jalapeño, 1 finely chopped green (spring) onion (white and tender green parts), 2 teaspoons minced fresh cilantro (fresh coriander), grated zest of 1 lime, 2 tablespoons fresh lime juice, ½ teaspoon salt, and ⅛ teaspoon freshly ground pepper.

Let stand for 15 minutes, adjust the seasonings, and serve or hold the salsa.

MAKES ABOUT 2 CUPS (16 FL OZ/500 ML)

Orange-Rosemary Salsa

Grilled chicken is a good partner for this salsa, which is full of unexpected flavors. If you like a spicier salsa, substitute extra-hot habanero chile for the jalapeño.

Peel and section 7 navel oranges: Using a chef's or serrated knife, remove a slice from the top and bottom of each orange to expose the flesh. Stand the orange on a flat end and, following the curve of the fruit, cut away all the peel and white pith from each orange. Working over a bowl, make a cut on each side of each segment to free it from the membrane, letting the segments and juice drop into the bowl.

Add ½ minced habanero or 1 minced jalapeño chile, ½ minced large shallot, 1 tablespoon finely chopped fresh rosemary, juice of ½ lime, ½ teaspoon salt, and ⅛ teaspoon freshly ground pepper to the bowl and mix together.

Let stand for 15 minutes, adjust the seasonings, and serve or hold the salsa.

MAKES ABOUT 2 CUPS (16 FL OZ/500 ML)

Grilled Red Pepper Coulis

Not all thick, rich sauces rely on butter for these characteristics. The French culinary term *coulis* refers to vegetable-based sauces that are nothing more than purées seasoned with only a few additional ingredients. Add too many items, and you risk muddling the bright flavor and color of the sauce's main ingredient.

2½ lb (1.25 kg) red bell peppers (capsicums) (about 5 large peppers)

1 tablespoon extra-virgin olive oil

1 tablespoon balsamic vinegar

¾ teaspoon salt

¼ teaspoon red pepper flakes

MAKES ABOUT 2 CUPS (16 FL OZ/500 ML)

CHEF'S TIP
If you don't want to fire up a grill, you can also roast whole, uncut peppers over the flame of a gas stove. Turn them with tongs until the skin is blistered and blackened on all sides; be careful not to let the flesh burn.

RECOMMENDED USES
As a sauce with grilled or poached fish or chicken breasts, as a flavoring for Mayonnaise (page 89), as a dip for raw vegetables, or as a spread for bruschetta.

1 Prepare a grill
Build a charcoal fire in an outdoor grill and let the fire burn until the coals are covered with white ash. Or, if using a gas grill, preheat it on high.

2 Prepare the bell peppers
Working with 1 bell pepper at a time, cut a 1-inch (2.5-cm) slice from the top and bottom of the pepper; cut out and discard the stem from the pepper top and reserve the top and bottom. Make a lengthwise cut to open the rest of the pepper and flatten it out. Cut out the ribs and seeds and discard.

3 Grill the bell peppers
Using a brush or paper towel, lightly oil the grill grate. Place the opened peppers, along with their tops and bottoms, shiny skin sides down, on the grill. Grill without turning, just until the skin is blistered and blackened, about 10 minutes. (There may be a few areas of the peppers that remain unblackened, but don't worry about them.) Do not let the flesh burn. Transfer the peppers to a bowl and let cool until they are easy to handle. Do not cover the peppers when cooling; the heat from the collected steam can make them too soft for this recipe.

4 Peel and purée the bell peppers
Using a small, sharp knife, remove and discard the skins from the peppers. Don't worry about removing every last bit of skin. In a food processor, process the peppers until relatively smooth. With the machine running, add the oil, vinegar, salt, and red pepper flakes. The coulis can be used at this point, but for a finer texture, strain it. Pour the coulis into a medium-mesh sieve set over a medium bowl. Using a rubber spatula, push the coulis through the sieve, scraping it firmly across the bottom of the sieve to ensure that all the sauce is pushed through. Scrape off any coulis that clings to the bottom of the sieve. Discard any solids left in the sieve.

5 Adjust the seasonings
Taste the coulis; it should taste primarily of red pepper, with a hint of smokiness from the grill. If it tastes dull, stir in a bit more vinegar, salt, or red pepper flakes until the flavors are nicely balanced.

6 Serve or store the coulis
Serve the coulis right away, or store it. Transfer the coulis to a covered container. Refrigerate for up to 3 days. Let the coulis come to room temperature before using. Whisk well before serving.

Peach Chutney

An amalgam of sweet, sour, savory, and spicy flavors that originated in India, chutney can be made and used in a variety of ways. Some recipes even call for unripe fruit. This chunky peach chutney, made from ripe and juicy peaches, captures the essence of summer with its full fruit flavor.

1 Shred the ginger
Using a vegetable peeler or paring knife, peel the ginger. Use the small shredding holes on a box grater-shredder to shred ½ cup (2 oz/60 g) ginger into a bowl, catching any juice.

2 Peel and cut the peaches
Bring a large saucepan three-fourths full of water to a boil over high heat. Fill a large bowl three-fourths full of ice water. Cut a shallow X in the blossom, or bottom, end of each peach. A few at a time, add the peaches to the boiling water. Cook just until the skins loosen, about 30 seconds. Using a slotted spoon, transfer the peaches to the ice water. Starting at the X, and using a paring knife, remove the skin from each peach. Halve each peach, remove the pit, and cut the halves into 1-inch (2.5-cm) pieces. (If using freestone peaches, the pits will be easy to remove. If using clingstone peaches, you may need to cut out the pits.)

3 Sauté the vegetables
Place a heavy-bottomed nonreactive saucepan over medium heat. Add the oil and heat until the surface of the oil just shimmers. Add the onion and cook, stirring often, until the onion is golden, about 5 minutes. Stir in the grated ginger, jalapeño, and garlic and cook until the garlic is fragrant, about 1 minute.

4 Simmer the chutney
Add the peaches, brown sugar, vinegar, and cinnamon stick. Cook, stirring often, until the peaches release their juices and the mixture comes to a boil. Reduce the heat to medium-low and cook the mixture, stirring often to avoid scorching, until the peaches are very tender and the juices are syrupy, 30–40 minutes. Remove the cinnamon stick and discard. Let cool completely. (You probably won't need to adjust the seasonings, as the flavors are quite bold.)

5 Use or store the chutney
Use the chutney right away, or store it. Transfer the cooled chutney to a covered container and refrigerate for up to 2 weeks. Serve the chutney chilled or at room temperature.

2 large knobs fresh ginger

3 lb (1.5 kg) ripe peaches, preferably freestone peaches

1 tablespoon canola oil

½ yellow onion, diced (page 30)

1 jalapeño chile, seeded and minced (page 40)

2 cloves garlic, minced (page 34)

½ cup (3½ oz/105 g) firmly packed light brown sugar

⅓ cup (3 fl oz/80 ml) cider vinegar

1 cinnamon stick, 3 inches (7.5 cm) long

MAKES ABOUT 3 CUPS (30 OZ/940 G)

CHEF'S TIP
It's best to make peach relishes with midseason fruit. Not only are they easier to peel, but they have a more vibrant color than early-season peaches.

RECOMMENDED USES
As a condiment for sliced ham, grilled or panfried chicken or pork chops; as an accompaniment to Indian dishes; as a sandwich spread.

Cranberry-Lime Relish

This tart and refreshing relish will enliven a tired palate, especially one exhausted by too many flavors on the holiday table. It is made with fresh cranberries accented by lime zest and maple sugar. The thick, chunky, bright-tasting relish is a welcome alternative to the jellied cranberry sauce often served during the holidays.

12 oz (375g) fresh cranberries

2 limes

1 cup (7 oz/220 g) firmly packed maple sugar or light brown sugar

MAKES ABOUT 2 CUPS (16 FL OZ/500 ML)

CHEF'S TIP
Although cranberries freeze well, do not use frozen cranberries for this recipe. Frozen cranberries lack the texture needed for raw preparations such as this relish.

1 **Rinse and sort the cranberries**
Place the cranberries in a colander and rinse under running cold water. Sort through the cranberries, discarding any that are shriveled or soft.

2 **Zest and juice the limes**
If you are not sure how to zest and juice citrus, turn to page 35. Grate the limes using a fine rasp grater to remove just the colored part of the peel, called the zest. Take care not to grate the white part below the peel, called the pith, as it can be bitter. Set the zest aside. Use a knife to cut the limes in half crosswise. Insert a citrus reamer into each half and turn to remove as much juice as possible. You'll need 3 tablespoons juice for this recipe.

3 **Process the ingredients**
In a food processor, combine the maple sugar and the 3 tablespoons lime juice. Using brief pulses, moisten the sugar thoroughly with the juice. Add the cranberries and lime zest. Pulse until the cranberries are coarsely chopped. Transfer the relish to a glass bowl. Cover and refrigerate the relish to blend the flavors, at least 2 hours.

4 **Adjust the seasonings**
Taste the relish; it should have the bright taste of cranberries accented by lime. If the relish is too tart, stir in a bit more sugar; if it lacks brightness, stir in a touch more lime juice until the flavors are nicely balanced.

5 **Serve or store the relish**
Serve the relish at room temperature or cover and refrigerate for at least 2 hours, and serve cold. You can store the relish in the refrigerator for up to 1 day.

RECOMMENDED USES
As a condiment for roasted or smoked turkey or ham.

Yogurt-Cucumber Sauce

This Greek dish, known as *tsatsiki*, consists of yogurt and cucumbers mixed to make an invigorating blend that many cooks consider to be among the best accompaniments to grilled lamb chops or kebabs. To create a naturally thick sauce, the excess liquid is drained from the yogurt and cucumbers. For extra thickness and authentic flavor, seek out dense, rich Greek-style yogurt, which needs no draining.

1 Drain the yogurt, if necessary
If you are not using Greek-style yogurt, you'll need to drain it to remove some of the liquid: Line a fine-mesh sieve with a double thickness of moistened cheesecloth (muslin), letting the excess cheesecloth hang over the sides. Place the sieve over a deep bowl: The bottom of the sieve should be at least 2 inches (5 cm) above the bottom of the bowl to allow room for draining. Spoon the yogurt into the sieve. Bring up the sides of the cheesecloth to cover the yogurt. Place a small plate on top to weigh down the yogurt. Refrigerate the bowl with the sieve and let the yogurt drain until about 1½ cups (¾ lb/375 g) thickened yogurt remains in the sieve, 3 to 4 hours. Discard the liquid in the bowl. Use a rubber spatula to transfer the yogurt to another bowl.

2 Prepare the cucumbers
Peel the cucumbers and cut them in half lengthwise. Using a teaspoon, scrape the seeds from the cucumbers. Shred the cucumbers on the large shredding holes of a box grater-shredder. Place the shredded cucumbers in a colander and mix with the salt. Let drain in the sink for 10 minutes to remove excess liquid from the cucumbers. This also helps to remove any trace of bitterness. Rinse the cucumbers under running cold water. A handful at a time, squeeze the cucumber in your fist to remove the excess liquid.

3 Mix the sauce ingredients
Add the cucumber to the bowl with the yogurt. Stir in the dill and garlic. Cover the bowl with plastic wrap and refrigerate until the sauce is chilled and the flavors are blended, at least 2 hours.

4 Adjust the seasonings
Stir in the pepper and taste the sauce. It should be creamy and nicely balanced, with no single flavor dominating. If the salt from the cucumbers is not enough, or the sauce tastes a little dull, stir in a bit more salt to bring out the flavors.

5 Serve or store the sauce
Serve the sauce right away, or store it. The sauce is delicious chilled, forming a pleasing contrast with hot foods. It can also be refrigerated for up to 2 days.

1½ cups plain Greek-style yogurt, or 3 cups (1½ lb/750 g) plain low-fat (not nonfat) yogurt

2 cucumbers

½ teaspoon salt

2 tablespoons chopped fresh dill or mint

2 cloves garlic, finely minced (page 34)

¼ teaspoon freshly ground black pepper

MAKES ABOUT 2 CUPS (16 FL OZ/500 ML)

CHEF'S TIP
The best yogurt sauces are made from natural yogurt without stabilizers or gelatin. After draining, the yogurt is creamy and smooth; those with additives turn out slightly gummy.

RECOMMENDED USES
As a sauce for poached salmon or grilled or sautéed lamb chops; as a dip for toasted pita wedges.

Horseradish-Chive Sauce

There are cooks who could not conceive of serving roast beef without thick and zesty horseradish sauce. Classic British recipes call for blending the pungent root with whipped cream, but I use sour cream for its wonderful tanginess and the fact that it holds its shape longer before melting in contact with hot meat.

1 piece fresh horseradish root, about 4 oz (125 g), or ¼ cup (2 oz/60 g) bottled horseradish

1 bunch fresh chives

2 cups (16 oz/500 g) sour cream

¼ teaspoon salt

¼ teaspoon freshly ground pepper

MAKES ABOUT 2 CUPS (16 FL OZ/500 ML)

CHEF'S TIP
The best time to find fresh horseradish root in markets is in the spring around the time of Passover; the pungent root is part of the holiday's traditional meal.

1 **Prepare the horseradish**
Using a sharp paring knife, remove the dark brown skin from the horseradish. Use the small shredding holes of a box grater-shredder or a fine rasp grater to shred ½ cup (1½ oz/45 g) horseradish. You will not use all of the horseradish root, but it is difficult to handle a smaller piece. You may want to avert your eyes slightly and avoid breathing the horseradish vapors, as they can be intense.

2 **Cut the chives**
Use kitchen shears or a chef's knife to cut the chives into pieces. I like to keep the pieces on the large side—about ¼ inch (6 mm)—to give the sauce some texture. You'll need about 3 tablespoons chopped chives.

3 **Mix the sauce**
In a bowl, stir together the sour cream and chives. Tasting as you go, gradually stir in enough horseradish to create a pleasingly intense sauce. Note that the flavors will bloom slightly as the sauce sits. Stir in the salt and pepper. Cover with plastic wrap and refrigerate to chill and blend the flavors, at least 4 hours. Remove the sauce from the refrigerator 1 hour before serving to take off the chill.

4 **Adjust the seasonings**
Just before serving, taste the sauce again; it should taste of pungent horseradish and oniony chives, with a cool, creamy contrast and tanginess from the sour cream. If the sauce tastes a little flat, stir in a bit more salt and pepper until the flavors are nicely balanced.

5 **Serve or store the sauce**
Serve the sauce right away, or store it. The sauce can be refrigerated in a covered container for up to 2 days.

RECOMMENDED USES
With roast beef, grilled or poached salmon, or corned beef; as a dip for potato chips; as a condiment for roast beef sandwiches; as a topping for baked potatoes.

Using Key Tools & Equipment

Sauces do not require an enormous collection of specialized equipment: You are likely to have the essential utensils and cookware in your kitchen already. In the instances where a less familiar or optional item is called for in this book, such as a flat roux whisk, you can be sure that it is a useful tool that will make cooking easier and more pleasurable, and not a white elephant. Select optional equipment according to the way you like to cook.

Choose heavy-gauge stainless-steel, anodized aluminum, enameled cast-iron, or lined copper cookware, with thick bottoms for even heating. Untreated aluminum and cast iron can react with eggs and with acidic ingredients like tomatoes or wine to give a sauce an off color or flavor.

Stockpots & Saucepans
A stockpot should be taller than it is wide (the narrower the stockpot, the less surface area of a liquid is exposed, slowing evaporation and improving

flavor); a 10- to 12-quart (10- to 12-l) stockpot is sufficient. For smaller yields, a 6-quart (6-l) saucepan or Dutch oven works well. A 2½- to 3-quart (2.5- to 3-l) straight-sided saucepan is a sound choice for whisked sauces such as béchamel. A saucepan with sloped sides is even better, because it has no corners for flour to collect and scorch.

Roasting, Frying & Sauté Pans
Roasting pans should have relatively low sides so that oven heat can circulate freely around the food. A smaller pan of

about 14 by 12 by 2 inches (35 by 30 by 5 cm) is a good all-purpose choice, but it's wise to have a larger pan, too, for big turkeys or roasts.

Straight-sided sauté pans provide plenty of depth for making pan sauces without splashing. Slope-sided sauté pans allow food to be tossed in the pan without tumbling out, which is useful when cooking diced vegetables. Uncoated pans are preferred for making pan sauces, as the browned bits that stick to them contribute to a flavorful sauce when they are deglazed with a liquid.

Spoons

A large slotted spoon or wide, flat, skimmer is used to skim the foam from the surface of a simmering stock or for removing large solids from a liquid. A large solid metal spoon is the preferred tool for degreasing stocks and defatting sauces. Wooden spoons are traditional for stirring sauces, as they allow you to judge the thickness of a sauce by how it coats the spoon. A flat-bottomed wooden spoon (or wooden spatula) will reach into the corners of a saucepan better than a rounded spoon and will deglaze a pan without scratching it.

Degreasing Cups

When you pour drippings from a roasting pan into a cup and let them stand for a few minutes, the fat will rise to the top. The ingenious design of the degreasing cup allows the flavorful juices to be poured off, leaving the fat behind. A 4-cup (32–fl oz/1-l) degreasing cup is best for large birds and roasts; choose a 2-cup (16–fl oz/500-ml) version for smaller meals.

Heatproof Silicone Spatulas

Developed to withstand heats up to 550°F (290°C) without melting, these innovative spatulas can be used to stir hot mixtures. They also perform the usual function of blending mixtures or scraping food cleanly from a bowl or pan.

Sieves

These tools help strain out unwanted particles of food from sauces. Two sizes, large and medium, allow for varying amounts of sauce. Fine- and medium-mesh sieves are needed for different textures of sauce. For an especially refined texture, a specialized cone-shaped sieve called a *chinois* (so called because it resembles an old-fashioned Chinese straw hat) does an unparalleled job.

Whisks

Whisks come in three styles, each designed for a specific task. A rounded balloon whisk does the best job of whipping air into whipped cream or beaten egg whites. An elongated French or egg whisk can be used directly in a saucepan to blend or smooth out a sauce. A flexible flat whisk is ideal for stirring together fat and flour in a sauté pan or roasting pan to make a roux.

Serving Equipment

A ladle helps you coat food with just the right amount of sauce. A well-equipped kitchen will have two sauceboats—a large one for a generous amount of holiday gravy, and a smaller one for other sauces.

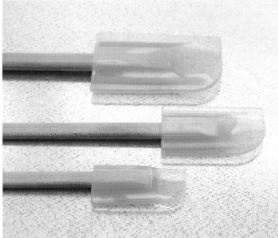

Puréeing Equipment

Some sauces get body from puréed ingredients. For low-tech puréeing, use a good-sized mortar and pestle (and elbow grease) to pound ingredients together. A mortar and pestle is the traditional way to make pesto. Electric options include food processors and blenders. A food processor fitted with the metal blade can be used for certain emulsified sauces, like mayonnaise, or for puréed pestos and chopped salsas. A blender does well with these first two jobs (pestos will be somewhat smoother), but is not recommended for salsa. A handheld electric mixer works well to whip cream. It also can be used to create emulsified sauces. Newer models come with both a whisk attachment and the traditional twin beaters. Any type of mixer can be used for this book.

Knives

For sauce making, the most useful knives are a chef's knife (for chopping vegetables and herbs and more) and a paring knife (to help remove the skins from tomatoes and the seeds from chiles, among other tasks). Kitchen scissors are useful for snipping herbs and cutting cheesecloth (muslin) or kitchen string for making a bouquet garni.

For chopping through poultry bones for stock, a heavy cleaver works best. (You can often use heavy-duty kitchen scissors for this job). Do not confuse it with the thin-bladed Asian cleaver, used for slicing meat and chopping vegetables.

A vegetable peeler and a serrated knife are nice to have, but are not essential. A slicer or utility knife with a thin, flexible blade is useful for filleting fish for bones to use in stock and for preparing other delicate ingredients. When using any knife, be sure to cut ingredients on a heavy wooden or plastic cutting board. To keep the boards from moving around on the counter as you work, place a folded damp paper towel or kitchen towel underneath the board.

Tools for Cheese and Citrus

The box grater-shredder has holes for shredding (larger, teardrop-shaped holes) and grating (small rasps). A fine rasp grater does double duty: It makes short work of finely grating hard cheeses and removing zest from citrus without digging into the bitter white pith. A citrus reamer, a rounded, ridged tool with a sharp point, is inserted into a citrus half and turned to easily extract the juice. It is a good tool for when you need small amounts of juice.

  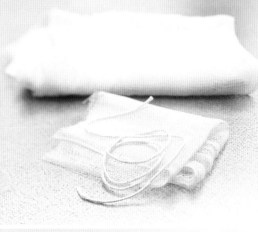

 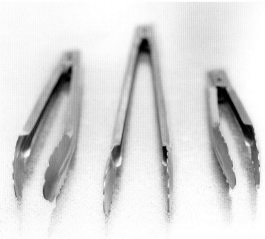 

Measuring Equipment

Different tools are needed to measure liquid and dry ingredients accurately. Liquids are poured into clear glass measuring cups. Often these cups are heatproof. Dry ingredients are measured in individual nested metal or plastic cups. Measuring spoons are used to measure small, leveled amounts of both dry and liquid ingredients. For more information on measuring sauce ingredients, turn to page 12.

Prep Bowls

Glass bowls or ceramic ramekins are good for holding small amounts of prepared ingredients; that way they are ready when it comes time to use them in a recipe. Glass bowls are convenient because they often come in sets, making stacking and storing in a small place possible, while ramekins do double duty, holding small servings of soufflés and desserts, among other foods.

Mixing Bowls

Tempered glass or stainless-steel bowls are preferred to plastic because the former do not retain flavors or grease. Placed over a saucepan of barely simmering water, a metal bowl can be used to create a double boiler for making hollandaise and other delicate sauces.

Tongs

Every kitchen needs a medium-sized pair of tongs, just right for turning food in a frying pan. Long tongs will help you reach into tall stockpots to move ingredients as needed. Short tongs are nice to have for manipulating small pieces of food in tight quarters, such as a small saucepan.

Spring-loaded tongs will help you keep a firm grip on the food.

Bundling Equipment

Inedible seasonings are tied up in a cheesecloth (muslin) bundle for easy removal at the end of cooking. To limit the absorption of the stock into the cheesecloth, rinse the cloth and then wring well before using. Use cotton kitchen string to tie the bundle.

Storage Supplies

Sauces made in advance should be refrigerated or frozen in airtight containers to keep out odors. If a sauce is hot, let it cool to room temperature before transferring it to a covered container. Place a piece of masking tape on the container and label with the name of the sauce and the date.

Glossary

ANCHOVY PASTE A purée of tiny, boldly flavored fish packed in small tubes. Add anchovy paste sparingly to sauces to lend a tangy, pungent, complex flavor.

APPLE CIDER, HARD Apple cider that has been allowed to ferment to yield a lightly sweet, alcoholic beverage.

ARUGULA Also known as rocket, these slender, green, deeply notched leaves have an appealing mild peppery taste.

BONES FOR STOCK In making meat stock, two kinds of bones are desirable: marrow-bones, which are typically leg and knuckle bones, and bony cuts from the neck or shin with meat still attached. The shin (or shank), which is the lower leg, is a naturally well-exercised muscle on any animal. The meat is flavorful and succulent and adds delicious flavor to stock with long, slow cooking. Marrowbones are not meaty but are rich in gelatin and marrow, the soft, rich, flavorful, and nutritious tissue lodged in the hollow center of bones.

BOUQUET GARNI A French term referring to a bundle of herbs and/or spices added to a stock or sauce to perfume it with flavor.

BOURBON Distilled primarily from corn, this slightly sweet whiskey takes its name from a county in Kentucky where it is made.

BUTTER
European style Made from fermented cream, European-style butter contains more butterfat than regular butter, giving it a pure, buttery flavor. It has also been treated to remove most of the liquid, giving it a denser and smoother texture than other types of butter.

Unsalted Unsalted butter allows the cook more control over the seasoning of a dish. In addition, unsalted butter tends to be fresher because salt acts as a preservative, lengthening the shelf life of butter at the supermarket. Refrigerate unsalted butter in its original wrapping for up to 6 weeks.

CAPERS Capers are the unopened flower buds of bushes native to the Mediterranean. The buds are dried, cured, and then usually packed in a vinegar brine. Capers are also sold packed in salt; rinse them thoroughly before using. Nonpareil capers, especially small capers from southern France, are considered by many cooks to be the finest.

CHEESES
Visiting a good cheese shop is a rewarding experience, since you'll be able to taste a variety of cheeses before you buy. Store cheeses in a warmer part of the refrigerator, like the door, wrapped in parchment (baking) or waxed paper rather than plastic, to allow them to breathe.

Cheddar First made in the village of Cheddar in England, this cheese is appreciated for its tangy, salty flavor, which ranges from mild to sharp, depending on age. Although naturally a creamy white, Cheddar is often dyed orange with annatto, a paste made from achiote seeds.

Cotija A flavorful Mexican cow's milk cheese suitable for grating. Look for it in Latin markets or large supermarkets that cater to a Mexican population.

Gorgonzola A cow's milk blue cheese from Italy with a moist, creamy texture and a pleasantly pungent flavor. When young, it is creamy, soft, and mildly pungent. This version is usually labeled Gorgonzola *dolcelatte* or *dolce*. Older, riper Gorgonzola, sometimes labeled *naturale*, has a much more pronounced flavor.

Gruyère This semifirm, dense, smooth cow's milk cheese is produced in Switzerland and France and is appreciated for its mild, nutty flavor and superior melting properties.

Parmigiano-Reggiano The "true" Parmesan cheese, this is an aged, hard grating cheese made from partially skimmed cow's milk. It has a a salty flavor and a rich, assertive fragrance. It is produced in the Emilia-Romagna region of Italy, and its rind is always labeled with its trademarked name, Parmigiano-Reggiano.

Pecorino Romano A pleasantly salty Italian sheep's milk cheese with a grainy texture, *pecorino romano* is primarily used for grating. It has a sharp, pungent flavor.

Roquefort France's premier blue cheese is made from sheep's milk. The interior is streaked with a delicate network of blue veins, the result of special mold cultures introduced during the ripening period. Pale, moist, and crumbly, Roquefort has a strong, salty, peppery flavor.

CHILES
Fresh chiles range in size from tiny to large, and in heat intensity from mild to fiery hot. Select firm, bright-colored chiles with blemish-free skins. To reduce the heat of a chile, remove the ribs and seeds, where the heat-producing compound, called *capsaicin*, resides. When working with hot chiles, wear a glove to avoid burning your skin, then wash your hands and any utensils thoroughly with hot, soapy water the moment you finish.

Chipotle A dried and smoked jalapeño chile (see below), with lots of flavor and lots of heat. These dark brown chiles are about 3 inches long and may be bought either dried or in cans or jars, packed in an oniony tomato mixture called adobo sauce.

Habanero Some consider this small fresh chile the hottest—and certainly its heat exceeds that of virtually every other commercially available chile—but it also has a lovely citrusy flavor. Habaneros can be green, orange, or red.

Jalapeño The jalapeño measures from 2–4 inches (5–10 cm) long, has a generous amount of flesh, and ranges from mildly hot to fiery. Green jalapeños are widely available, but you can sometimes find red ones, the ripened form, which are slightly sweeter than the unripened chiles.

CHILI SAUCE Not to be confused with Asian chile sauces, this American-style sauce is a mild ketchuplike blend of tomatoes, chili powder, onions, green bell peppers (capsicums), vinegar, sugar, and spices. Look for chili sauce near the condiments in the supermarket.

CORNSTARCH Cornstarch (cornflour) is a highly refined, silky powder made from corn kernels and used to thicken sauces.

Cornstarch lends a glossy sheen to sauces thickened with it, unlike those sauces that are thickened with flour. Cornstarch has nearly twice the thickening power of flour.

EGGS Eggs are sometimes used uncooked or partially cooked in sauces. All eggs have a small chance of being infected with salmonella or other bacteria, and consuming them raw can lead to food poisoning. This risk is of most concern to young children, elders, pregnant women, and anyone with a compromised immune system. If you have health and safety concerns, do not consume raw eggs, and seek out a pasteurized egg product to replace them. Eggs can be made safe by heating them to a temperature of 160°F (71°C) or to 140°F (60°C) for 3½ minutes. Note that poached and soft-boiled eggs do not reach this temperature.

GARLIC When buying garlic, choose plump, firm heads with no brown discolorations. (A tinge of purple is fine, even desirable.) Always take care not to cook garlic beyond a light golden color, or it can taste harsh.

GHERKINS Also called cornichons, these small, tart, crisp pickles are prepared with cucumbers that are specifically grown to be picked while still very small.

GINGER A refreshing combination of spicy and sweet, ginger adds a lively note to many dishes. Hard and knobby fresh ginger has thin, pale brown skin. Although called a root, it is actually a rhizome, or underground stem. Select fresh ginger that is firm and heavy and has smooth, unbroken skin.

HERBS
Using fresh herbs is one of the best things you can do to improve your cooking. Dried herbs do have their place; they are useful in dry rubs and certain other preparations, but fresh herbs usually bring brighter flavors to a dish. Many herbs are very easy to grow, even if all the room you have for them is a sunny porch or windowsill; they tend to be hardy plants. Wrap fresh herbs in damp paper towels, then wrap in a plastic bag and refrigerate for 3 to 5 days.

Basil Used in kitchens throughout the Mediterranean and in Southeast Asia, basil tastes faintly of anise and cloves. Many different varieties of this tender herb are available, including common sweet Italian basil and reddish purple Thai basil with its distinct licorice flavor.

Bay Elongated gray-green leaves used to flavor sauces and other dishes, imparting a slightly sweet, citrusy, nutty flavor. Usually sold dried, bay leaves should be removed from a dish before serving, as they are leathery and can have sharp edges.

Chives These slender, hollow, grasslike leaves are used to give an onionlike flavor to sauces, without the bite. Chives do not take well to long cooking; they lose flavor and crispness and turn a dull grayish green.

Cilantro Also called fresh coriander and Chinese parsley, cilantro is a distinctly flavored herb used extensively in Mexican, Asian, Indian, Latin, and Middle Eastern cuisines. Cilantro's pungent aroma and bright astringent taste are distinctive. Use it sparingly at first until you are familiar with its flavor. It is best when added at the end of cooking; its flavor disappears during long exposure to heat. When shopping, do not confuse cilantro and flat-leaf (Italian) parsley, which both have delicate, scalloped leaves and are easily mistaken for each other.

Dill This herb has fine, feathery leaves with a distinct aromatic flavor. Dill is common in Greek- and American-style sauces.

Mint This refreshing herb is available in many varieties, with spearmint the most common. It is used to flavor a broad range of different types of sauces, and is a favorite seasoning in Southeast Asian and Middle Eastern kitchens.

Parsley Two types of parsley are commonly available: curly-leaf parsley and flat-leaf, or Italian, parsley. Many cooks favor flat-leaf parsley for its cleaner, more pronounced flavor. Tender parsley has a clean, fresh taste that pairs well with a wide range of foods.

Rosemary This woody Mediterranean herb, with leaves like pine needles, has an assertive flavor that pairs well with chicken, beef, lamb, many vegetables, and seafood, but it should be used in moderation.

Sage These soft, gray-green leaves are sweet and aromatic. Sage pairs well with sauces for poultry, pork, and winter squash, and is a common addition to Northern Italian dishes.

Tarragon With its slender, deep green leaves and elegant, aniselike scent, tender tarragon is among the most common herbs in the French garden. Along with chives, parsley, and chervil, it is an essential ingredient in the mixture known as *fines herbes* and is frequently used with fish and chicken.

Thyme Tiny green leaves on thin stems, this herb is a mild, all-purpose seasoning. Its floral, earthy flavor complements meats, fish, vegetables, and salads. If a large amount is needed, gently pull the leaves backward off the stem with one motion. When the thyme stems are young and still very soft, you can chop them along with the leaves, but more mature stems will be woody.

HOISIN SAUCE This spicy, slightly sweet, brownish red sauce is made from fermented soybeans enlivened with five-spice powder, garlic, and dried chile. It is widely available in bottles and jars in the Asian section of most supermarkets. Once opened, it will keep indefinitely in the refrigerator. Hoisin sauce is a versatile ingredient that can be used alone or added to other sauces and glazes to contribute flavor and color.

HORSERADISH A thick, gnarled root of a plant in the cabbage family. Fresh horseradish root has a refreshing, spicy bite, and must be peeled first to reveal the creamy white, edible flesh below the brown skin. Look for fresh horseradish in the produce section of a specialty-food store or well-stocked supermarket.

HOT-PEPPER SAUCE A splash of hot-pepper sauce adds zip to sauces. There are countless varieties of hot-pepper sauce made with a rainbow of pepper colors and heat levels, so allow yourself the opportunity to experiment and find one you especially like.

INSTANT-READ THERMOMETER This type of thermometer is inserted into foods toward the end of the cooking period to test for doneness. Instant-read thermometers are more accurate than probe-type thermometers, and make a smaller hole in meat or poultry, thus releasing less juice.

LEEKS A sweet and mild-flavored member of the onion family, a leek is long and cylindrical with a pale white root end and dark green leaves. The green leaves are tough; most recipes use only the white and sometimes the pale green parts. Select firm, unblemished, small or medium leeks. Because leeks grow partly underground, often in sandy soil, grit can be lodged between the layers of their leaves. Be sure to clean them thoroughly before using.

MADEIRA A fortified wine from Portugal, made in versions from dry to sweet.

MANGOES Juicy, sweet-fleshed fruit native to India and now cultivated in many other tropical regions. When shopping for ripe mangoes, choose fruits that are aromatic at their stem end and have uniformly smooth skin. Ripe mangoes should give slightly to gentle pressure.

MAPLE SUGAR Available at natural-foods stores, maple sugar is made by boiling sap from the maple tree until nearly all the moisture has evaporated. It is a delicious substitute for brown sugar.

MEDALLIONS Medallions are round, boneless, tender cuts of beef, pork, lamb, or veal from the rib or loin sections of the animal. Medallions are perfect for quick grilling or sautéing. Medallions are also called *noisettes*.

MOLASSES A by-product of refining sugar, molasses is available in jars in 3 different types: light, dark, and blackstrap. Molasses is used to sweeten and deepen the flavor of some sauces, such as barbecue sauce.

MUSHROOMS, SHIITAKE These, the most popular mushrooms in Japan, are now widely cultivated. Fresh shiitakes should be buff to dark brown in color and have smooth, plump caps. Remove the tough stems before using.

MUSTARD
At its simplest, prepared mustard is a mixture of ground mustard seed and water. But this basic paste, available smooth or coarse grained, has been refined around the world by adding a number of flavorful ingredients.

Creole A coarse mustard common in New Orleans, it features brown mustard seeds, vinegar, garlic, and bold spices.

Dijon Originating in Dijon, France, this silky smooth and slightly tangy mustard contains brown or black mustard seeds, white wine, and herbs.

Spicy brown Typical in American-style delicatessens, spicy brown mustard is a hearty alternative to yellow mustard. It is made from brown mustard seeds, sugar, vinegar, and spices.

NOISETTES See Medallions.

NONREACTIVE A term used to describe a pan or dish made of or lined with a material that will not react with acidic ingredients. This includes stainless steel, enamel, ceramic, and glass.

NUTS An essential ingredient in virtually every cuisine, nuts provide richness, flavor, body, and crunch to a variety of dishes. In the world of sauces, they're most often found in pounded, pestolike mixtures. Since they contain high amounts of oils, nuts should be stored in the refrigerator to prevent them from turning rancid. There they will keep for 3 to 6 months.

Almonds Found inside the pit of a dry fruit related to peaches, almonds have a pointed, oval shape and a delicate fragrance. They are available whole, sliced, blanched (with skins removed), and slivered, and salted, roasted, or natural.

Pine nuts These are the seeds of pine trees, where they can be found nestled in the cones. They are small, rich nuts with an elongated, slightly tapered shape and resinous, sweet flavor.

Walnuts The furrowed, double-lobed meat of the walnut has a rich, assertive flavor. The most common variety is the English walnut, which has a light brown shell that cracks easily. Walnuts are sold whole, as halves, and as pieces.

OIL
Cooking oils play an essential role in the kitchen. The other ingredients and the heat

requirements of a recipe usually suggest which oil is most appropriate to use. As a general rule, choose less refined, more flavorful oils for uncooked uses, and refined, less flavorful oils for coating foods and for cooking.

Asian sesame Pressed from toasted sesame seeds, this deep amber–colored oil has a rich, nutty flavor. It is best used sparingly as a seasoning.

Canola This neutral-flavored oil, notable for its monounsaturated fats, is recommended for general cooking.

Olive Olive oil contributes a delicate, fruity flavor to dishes. Deeply flavorful extra-virgin olive oil is used to best advantage uncooked as a seasoning. Virgin and pure olive oils are not as fragrant as extra-virgin, but are good, less-expensive cooking oils with subtle flavor.

Soybean A neutral-flavored oil pressed from soybeans, with a high smoke point.

Walnut Rich-tasting, deep brown nut oil imported from France or Italy. Walnut oil turns rancid easily and should be bought in small quantities from a high-volume purveyor, then stored in the refrigerator. Walnut oil has a very low smoke point, so it should not be used for frying.

OLIVES, KALAMATA Almond-shaped, purplish-black, rich, and meaty, the Kalamata olive is brine-cured and then packed in oil or vinegar.

ONIONS
Green Also known as scallions or spring onions, green onions are the immature shoots of the bulb onion, with a narrow white base that has not yet begun to swell and long, flat green leaves. They are mild in flavor and can be enjoyed raw, stir-fried, grilled, braised, or chopped as a garnish for sauces, soups, and other dishes.

White This variety is milder and less sweet than the yellow onion.

Yellow The yellow globe onion is the common, all-purpose onion sold in supermarkets. Yellow onions are usually too harsh for serving raw, but they become rich and sweet when cooked.

PEPPERCORNS, GREEN Green peppercorns are black peppercorns that are harvested while still unripe. Typically packed in brine, they are a piquant addition to sauces.

POTATOES, NEW Immature potatoes, usually of the round red or round white variety. (Be aware that not all small red and white potatoes are new). Most often available in spring and early summer, new potatoes have thin skins, are low in starch, and will not keep long.

PUMPKIN SEEDS Also called *pepitas*, pumpkin seeds are a common ingredient in Mexican cuisine. They are medium green and have a delicate nutty flavor, which intensifies with roasting. Look for pumpkin seeds in in Latin markets or large supermarkets that cater to a Mexican population.

SALT Table salt is usually amended with iodine and with additives that enable it to flow freely. Sea salt and kosher salt are preferred by serious cooks.

Kosher salt Usually free of additives, this salt has large, coarse flakes that are easy to grasp between fingertips. In addition, kosher salt is used more liberally than regular table salt or sea salt because it does not taste as salty—you'll need almost twice as much.

Sea salt Available in coarse or fine grains, this salt also rarely contains additives, and is produced naturally by evaporation. The taste of each variety is influenced by the location where it was made. Sea-salt grains are the shape of hollow, flaky pyramids, which dissolve more readily than kosher salt.

SHALLOTS These small members of the onion family look like large cloves of garlic covered with papery bronze or reddish skin. Shallots have white flesh streaked with purple, a crisp texture, and a flavor more subtle than that of onions.

SOY SAUCE This pungent, salty sauce, made from fermented soybeans, wheat, and water, comes in various types and textures. Reduced-sodium soy sauce, while still high in sodium, has about half the sodium of regular soy sauce, allowing the cook more control over the seasoning of a dish.

TOMATILLOS Literally "little tomatoes," these are actually not related to the tomato. Firm and green, the tomatillo has a tart, citrusy flavor when raw; roasting tempers the sharpness and sweetens the flesh. Choose firm specimens with tightly clinging husks; remove the papery husks and rinse away the sticky residue before using.

TOMATO PASTE A dense purée made from slow-cooked tomatoes that have been strained and reduced to a deep red concentrate. Tomato paste is sold in tubes, tins, and jars.

TOMATOES, PLUM These egg-shaped tomatoes, also known as Roma tomatoes, have meaty, flavorful flesh prized particularly for sauce making.

VINEGAR

Many types are available, made from a variety of red or white wines or, like cider vinegar and rice vinegar, from fruits and grains. Vinegars are further seasoned by infusing them with fresh herbs, fruit, garlic, or other flavorful ingredients.

Balsamic Aged vinegar made from unfermented grape juice of white Trebbiano grapes. Balsamic may be aged briefly, for only 1 year, or for as long as 75 years; the vinegar slowly evaporates and grows sweeter and mellower. Balsamic vinegar is a specialty of Italy's Emilia-Romagna region, chiefly the town of Modena.

Cider A fruity vinegar made from apples and used in many traditional American recipes.

Raspberry Made by steeping raspberries in vinegar, resulting in sweet flavor and deep raspberry color. It is used often in French cuisine, particularly for vinaigrettes.

Red wine A pantry staple carried in most supermarkets, red wine vinegar is created by allowing red wine to ferment naturally over a period of months.

Rice Produced from fermented rice and widely used in Asian cuisines. It adds a slight acidity to cooked dishes and makes an excellent dressing for delicate greens. For cooking, make sure you find unseasoned rice vinegar.

Sherry Full-bodied vinegar possessing a nutty taste. It is especially good on vegetables and in salad dressings.

Tarragon Made by steeping fresh tarragon in vinegar, resulting in a vinegar infused with a sweet, aniselike flavor.

White wine A pantry staple carried in most supermarkets, white wine vinegar is created by allowing white wine to ferment naturally over a period of months.

WASABI Similar to horseradish, this Japanese root is commonly sold in two forms, as a green powder and as a green paste. It adds pungent flavor to any dish.

WHITE PEPPER Made from black peppercorns that have had their skins removed before the berries are dried, white pepper is often less aromatic and more mild in flavor than black pepper. It is favored in the preparation of light-colored sauces and dips.

WORCESTERSHIRE SAUCE A traditional English condiment, Worcestershire sauce is an intensely flavored, savory blend of varied ingredients, including molasses, soy sauce, garlic, onion, and anchovies.

YOGURT, GREEK STYLE

Greek-style yogurt, which is often made from whole milk, is already quite thick and will not need to be drained. Look for it in the dairy section of natural-foods stores and many supermarkets.

ZEST The colored portion of citrus peel, which is rich in flavorful oils. The white portion of the peel, called the pith, is bitter. When choosing citrus intended for zesting, look for organic fruit, since pesticides concentrate in thin skins of fruits and vegetables.

Index

A

Aioli (Garlic Mayonnaise), 94
ALMONDS
    about, 136
    Pistou, 115
Anchovy paste, 134
Apple cider, hard, 134
ARTICHOKES
    boiling, 26
    sauces for, 89, 97, 103
ARUGULA
    about, 134
    Arugula Pesto, 115
Asian Vinaigrette, 103
ASPARAGUS
    sauces for, 85, 97, 103
    steaming, 26

B

Balsamic Beurre Blanc, 99
Balsamic vinegar, 137
BARBECUE SAUCE
    Chipotle Barbecue Sauce, 71
    Georgia-Style Barbecue Sauce, 70
    Ginger Barbecue Sauce, 71
    Kansas City–Style Barbecue Sauce, 68
    Memphis-Style Barbecue Sauce, 70
    South Carolina–Style Mustard Sauce, 70
    Texas-Style Barbecue Sauce, 71
BASIL
    about, 112, 135
    Basil Pesto, 109–13
    Pesto with Walnuts and Pecorino, 114
Bay leaves, 135
BEANS
    Black Bean and Corn Salsa, 118
    sauces for, 101, 104
    steaming, 26
Béarnaise Sauce, 87
BÉCHAMEL SAUCE, 61–62
    Cheddar Sauce, 63
    Gorgonzola Sauce, 63
    Mornay Sauce, 63
BEEF
    Brown Meat Stock, 20–21
    grilling, 27
    panfrying, 26
    Pan Gravy, 55–59
    roasting, 27
    sauces for, 47–50, 51, 52, 53, 63, 67, 71, 73, 74,
        87, 99, 104, 114, 117, 128

BELL PEPPERS
    Grilled Red Pepper Coulis, 120
    Red Bell Pepper Hollandaise Sauce, 86
BEURRE BLANC, 97–98
    Balsamic Beurre Blanc, 99
    Beurre Rouge, 99
    Citrus Beurre Blanc, 99
Beurre Rouge, 99
Black Bean and Corn Salsa, 118
Blender Hollandaise Sauce, 87
Blenders, 132
Blender Vinaigrette, 102
BLUE CHEESE
    about, 134
    Blue Cheese Compound Butter, 104
    Gorgonzola Sauce, 63
    Roquefort, Sherry, and Walnut Vinaigrette, 102
Bones for stock, 134
Bordelaise sauce, 74
Bouquet garni, 23, 40, 134
BOURBON
    about, 134
    Bourbon Pan Sauce, 53
BOWLS
    mixing, 133
    prep, 133
BROCCOLI
    sauces for, 61, 63, 85, 97
    steaming, 26
Broken sauces, fixing, 42–43
Brown Butter–Caper Sauce, 77
Brown Meat Stock, 20–21
Brown mustard, spicy, 136
Brown Poultry Stock, 18–19
Brown Sauce, Modern, 67
Brussels sprouts, 97
Bundling, 133
BUTTER. *See also* Beurre Blanc; Hollandaise
    Sauce
    Brown Butter–Caper Sauce, 77
    clarifying, 36, 81
    Compound Butter, 104
    European-style, 11, 134
    measuring, 12
    mounting sauces with, 13, 14, 41
    unsalted, 11, 134

C

Canola oil, 136
CAPERS
    about, 134
    Brown Butter–Caper Sauce, 77

    Rémoulade, 95
    Tartar Sauce, 95
Carrots, dicing, 32
CAULIFLOWER
    sauces for, 61, 63, 85
    steaming, 26
CELERY
    dicing, 33
    removing strings from, 33
CHEDDAR CHEESE
    about, 134
    Cheddar Sauce, 63
CHEESE. *See also individual varieties*
    tools for, 132
    varieties of, 11, 134
Cheesecloth, 133
CHICKEN
    Brown Poultry Stock, 18–19
    grilling, 27
    panfrying, 26
    Pan Gravy, 55–59
    Pan Sauce, 47–51
    roasting, 27
    sauces for, 47–50, 51, 52, 53, 67, 68, 70, 74, 77,
        103, 115, 119, 120
    White Stock, 22–23
CHILES. *See also individual chiles*
    Chipotle Barbecue Sauce, 71
    reducing heat of, 134
    Tomato Salsa, 117
    varieties of, 134
    working with, 40, 134
Chili sauce, 134
CHIPOTLE CHILES
    about, 134
    Chipotle Barbecue Sauce, 71
CHIVES
    about, 135
    Horseradish-Chive Sauce, 128
Chutney, Peach, 123
Cider vinegar, 137
CILANTRO
    about, 135
    Cilantro Pesto, 115
CITRUS FRUITS. *See also individual fruits*
    Citrus Beurre Blanc, 99
    juicing, 35
    tools for, 132
    zesting, 35, 137
Compound Butter, 104
Cooking times, 13
Corn and Black Bean Salsa, 118

FREE PRESS

A Division of Simon & Schuster, Inc.
1230 Avenue of the Americas
New York, NY 10020

WILLIAMS-SONOMA

Founder & Vice-Chairman Chuck Williams

WELDON OWEN INC.

Chief Executive Officer John Owen
President and Chief Operating Officer Terry Newell
Chief Financial Officer Christine E. Munson
Vice President International Sales Stuart Laurence
Creative Director Gaye Allen
Publisher Hannah Rahill
Senior Editor Jennifer Newens
Editor Sarah Putman Clegg
Editorial Assistant Juli Vendzules
Art Director Kyrie Forbes
Designers Marisa Kwek and Adrienne Aquino
Production Director Chris Hemesath
Color Manager Teri Bell
Production and Reprint Coordinator Todd Rechner
Food Stylist William Smith
Prop Stylist Nancy Micklin Thomas
Assistant Food Stylist Matthew Vohr
Assistant Food Stylist and Hand Model Brittany Williams
Photographer's Assistant Amy Sessler

PHOTO CREDITS

Mark Thomas, all photography, except the following:
Bill Bettencourt: Pages 34, 36 (ginger sequence), 40 (chile sequence),
112, 113 (above), 131 (top left, top right), and 132 (bottom right).

THE MASTERING SERIES

Conceived and produced by Weldon Owen Inc.
814 Montgomery Street, San Francisco, CA 94133
Telephone: 415 291 0100 Fax: 415 291 8841

In collaboration with Williams-Sonoma, Inc.
3250 Van Ness Avenue, San Francisco, CA 94109

A WELDON OWEN PRODUCTION
Copyright © 2005 by Weldon Owen Inc. and Williams-Sonoma Inc.

All rights reserved, including the right of reproduction in whole or in part
in any form.

FREE PRESS and colophon are registered trademarks of Simon & Schuster, Inc.

For information regarding special discounts for bulk purchases,
please contact Simon & Schuster Special Sales at 1 800 456 6798 or
business@simonandschuster.com

Set in ITC Berkeley and FF The Sans.

Color separations by Embassy Graphics.
Printed and bound in China by SNP Leefung Printers Limited.

First printed in 2005.

10 9 8 7 6 5 4 3 2

Library of Congress Cataloging-in-Publication data is available.

ISBN–13: 978-0-7432-6737-3
ISBN–10: 0-7432-6737-0

ACKNOWLEDGMENTS

Weldon Owen wishes to thank the following people for their generous
support in producing this book: Desne Ahlers, Melinda Casidy,
Ken DellaPenta, Emily Jahn, Karen Kemp, Hilmar Koch, Renée Myers,
Cynthia Scheer, Sharon Silva, Chris & Jennifer Stark, Kate Washington,
and Sharron Wood.

A NOTE ON WEIGHTS AND MEASURES

All recipes include customary U.S. and metric measurements. Metric conversions are based on
a standard developed for these books and have been rounded off. Actual weights may vary.